# Growth Units

*Learn to Calculate Customer Acquisition Cost, Lifetime Value, and Why Businesses Behave the Way They Do.*

# Paul Orlando

*To my lovely wife, Susan Joan.*

# Contents

# Introduction

For over five years I have hung a peculiar sign in my office at the University of Southern California. It is a picture of a monkey with the caption "Remember Santiago." A peculiar sign and yet probably only one percent of people who visit ever ask me about it. However, that sign sums up much of what I think about building new businesses. (If you have read an earlier work of mine called *Startup Sacrilege* then you are already familiar with Santiago.)

And actually, once you know the story behind the monkey (I'm not giving the story away) you begin to see it everywhere (the story, not the monkey). But the real surprise for me about the sign is that while unusual, almost no one asks about it. But that's the way the world is. Even when they see the sign, few people realize what's there for them to see.

So this is a book about noticing what goes on beneath the surface. You can get there by asking questions, which we'll do throughout the entire book. Importantly, I will leave you with helpful calculations, extensive examples, metrics from many companies and industries, and frameworks to apply to new situations.

A lot goes into business success. But the focus of this book is on ways companies gain customers and earn money from them. I don't mean this in the marketing sense, but rather the way customer acquisition and lifetime value make businesses successful -- or not.

# It Depends...

"It depends." Those are two frustrating words. But the important and interesting questions are often complex, rather than objectively yes or no. The book will be a guide to figure out what specific situations depend upon and what to do about it. But the "it depends" will remain because what makes sense for your business might not make sense for mine.

Decisions aren't made in a vacuum and data can be stressed or suppressed depending on the story it tells. But I'm avoiding that (big) side of business decisions here.

I ended up writing this book because of several experiences that changed the way I think about building businesses and working with entrepreneurs. First, I have operated startup accelerators for eight years. I started by co-founding the first funded startup accelerator in Hong Kong. Later I was hired to build the student, alumni, faculty, and staff startup incubator at the University of Southern California in Los Angeles (USC). Along the way I also helped lead a startup accelerator in Rome that was run with input from the Vatican (true story). I've now selected hundreds of startups for my programs and have seen these very different companies up close. Along the way I've helped a lot of other startup programs and corporates, too. While many things are different depending on what you're doing and where you are, many things are also the same.

In a more formal setting, I also teach entrepreneurship classes at USC, including a class I created that is dedicated to the subject of how businesses grow. That class is not about short-lived growth hacking techniques (and neither is this book) and instead is about the fundamentals that will serve you well regardless of when you apply them. It soon became a popular class that draws from a wide range of students – everything from majors in business, engineering, design, and even a couple lost PhDs. Many students go on to be hired in a growth role or to use the techniques on their own businesses. Before any of this I also ran a startup in New York, worked in management consulting, and in tech product development in Asia.

The years working with startups and teaching gave me experience to know where businesspeople often ran into problems. The experience also demonstrated the need for a hands-on and analytic approach to figuring out how to step through specific business problems. My goal is that through asking questions and using some math, you will come to intuitively understand these principles. To provide examples I show 15 industry case studies to demonstrate different (and often strange) business behavior.

Feel free to say hi about the *Growth Units* topic. I'll add you to an infrequent email list if you like: paul@startupsunplugged.com.

# What You Will Learn

*What are the fundamentals of building a sustainable product? How do we improve these fundamentals? Introducing the unit economics of customer acquisition cost and lifetime value.*

In this book you will:
- Understand and calculate Customer Acquisition Cost in a variety of scenarios,
- Understand and calculate Lifetime Value in a variety of scenarios,
- See examples of Unit Economics, Lifetime Value, and Customer Acquisition Cost from different businesses and industries.

Since the book is about ways businesses grow, I called it *Growth Units*.

Chapters start with summary questions. In the Appendixes are definitions of terms and the referred to sources.

I like to bring out examples from both tech and non-tech companies. As a percentage of business and economic value, startups and tech are still small. I hope that this broader view will help you see how principles of *Growth Units* apply in everyday businesses you see when walking down the street to buy a cup of coffee.

Rather than use academic formulas, I show straightforward ones and spreadsheets that you can build. This is meant to be a useful text with examples -- but not a textbook.

One other note. Based on where you are in your business or learning, the concepts in this book may not be your current priority. Other matters, such as hiring, communication, sales, or fundraising may be more urgent at the time. But you will inevitably have to return to the concepts in this book. These concepts are fundamentals of business sustainability.

### Introducing Unit Economics and Why We Should Care
Unit economics are the direct revenues and costs associated with serving a customer with a unit of output. A cup of coffee, a month of a subscription service, a rideshare trip. One unit sold, one unit bought.

One part of unit economics is contribution margin, or the financial contribution selling one unit of a product or service makes to the business.

Taken across all sales the business makes, this would be gross profit (or as a percentage, gross margin). I mostly use business operator (rather than accounting) terms in this book and keep the examples as direct as possible. You'll see me reference each of these terms at different times.

If you sell that cup of coffee for $4 and it costs $1 to produce, your contribution margin is then $3 (or 75%).

Contribution margin is a factor of price and cost. But both price and cost can change.

Price could change as much as you want. Your volume of purchases will however be impacted as you move prices up or down. Do not assume that purchase volume always goes down as price goes up. That's a textbook assumption rather than a real world outcome (and one that the coffee industry learned years ago). Also do not assume that you want to maximize units sold. You may want to maximize market share or may choose to maximize profit, for example.

Your costs can also change as you decide to use different methods and materials, become more or less efficient, purchase at different volumes, have access to different rates for borrowing, types of talent or tech, or have to compete for resources.

These inputs only tell part of the story. We can figure out how much a company earns each time an item is sold, but is the total volume enough to cover other non-gross margin costs like rent and employee compensation? Are the price and cost decisions setting up the company for future problems in market share and customer retention? How much does it cost to acquire a new customer? How many times do customers buy? Over what time period do they buy? We'll get to all of this in detail but here's a brief overview.

If a customer buys the above coffee (price of $4, cost to produce of $1) a total of five times before leaving, then their Lifetime Value (LTV) is $15 ($3 in contribution margin X 5 purchases = $15). And if it costs you $4 to acquire that customer through marketing (the Customer Acquisition Cost, or CAC), then your Lifetime Value to Customer Acquisition Cost ratio is $15 : $4 or 3.75. (That's often considered good.)

Understanding unit economics, LTV, and CAC are important to build a sustainable business and one capable of growing. But calculating your unit economics can be surprisingly difficult. Many early-stage businesspeople avoid the analysis altogether until they get to the point of hiring a growth or data analysis team. If you use the frameworks in this book, you'll understand the unit economics of other companies (which may be different from yours) and how you might apply that framework in your own business.

If you understand this for your own business, you'll have a fighting chance. You'll also be able to observe other businesses and, with some thinking and maybe some research, will be able to estimate their own unit economics. If you can estimate CAC, and LTV for competitors you will understand their strengths and weaknesses.

These two simple sounding terms are actually quite complex once you dive into how they work. If you don't understand CAC, and LTV for your own business or competitors, you will fly blind as you try to navigate your way to new growth milestones.

CAC and LTV usually vary in precision depending on how much the business knows about its customers.

Differences in the way that CAC and LTV work also determine how certain we can be about them.

Customer Acquisition Cost, as the name implies, is incurred up front when you acquire a new customer, and before the customer generates revenue for you. But Lifetime Value is often only generated over time, and often with a delay, rather than as a one-off payment. That means that we often understand CAC before we understand LTV. This can cause problems.

To get better accuracy, we can also dive into each channel for customer acquisition and each customer segment for LTV. We can test different channels for acquisition and rate them on cost and associated LTV. We can look at payback periods. The list goes on.

Throughout *Growth Units* we'll look at ways to deal with uncertainty and how to make estimates better, but we'll always go with "approximately right" over "precisely wrong."

Throughout, remember that it may actually be logical for businesses to get themselves into tactical binds even if they know that the bind is coming. These are just a few of the factors at play.

Let's first dive into understanding CAC better.

# Customer Acquisition Cost (CAC)

*What is a customer (and why isn't this such a simple question)? What is CAC? Why spend effort to calculate CAC? What should understanding CAC help a business do?*

A customer pays a business for what they sell. If they aren't paying, they aren't a customer.

There are usually many more people who don't want or need what a specific business provides. Those are **non-customers**. There are also people who do want what is provided, but just don't know it exists or who haven't converted to purchase yet. Those are **potential customers**.

An easy framework of an ideal, or "earlyvangelist" customer (the easiest ones to consider, especially early on) comes from Steve Blank, in *Four Steps to the Epiphany*. An ideal customer has the following list of characteristics, with the higher numbered ones being stronger determinants of likelihood to be an ideal customer. The assumption is that if the customer is high on the list (higher numbers), they also have some of the lower numbered qualities.
1. They have a problem (that you potentially solve),
2. They know that they have the problem,
3. They are looking for a solution to the problem,
4. They have hacked together a solution to the problem,
5. They have or can acquire a budget to solve the problem.

Typically, the vast mass of humanity does not have a problem that a specific business solves. They are not even at number one in the list above. This comes as a surprise to many early-stage founders, but believe me it is true. The claim, "but everyone would want this… it's just so cool!" does not help.

Even more frustrating, those who do have the problem your business solves and the product you produce often do not realize that they have the problem in the first place.

There are also businesses that have unpaid users, who attract paying customers to the business (such as advertising platforms like Facebook). Here you have to remember that from the business' point of view, the purpose of these free users is to provide a market for their paid customers to advertise to.

CAC metrics include variables of the cost to reach potential customers, conversion rate, cycle time, time to payback, and more. CAC can be made more specific by calculating it across different segments and connecting it to LTV.

For now, know that CAC is the measure of the cost to start a relationship with a new customer. And while customer acquisition can be free, much of the time it costs something.

# Customer Acquisition Cost an Unhelpful Way (A Way You Often See It)

*We'll look at common unhelpful ways CAC is calculated and why they are not helpful.*

Let's show how CAC is often casually shown -- what I'll call **the unhelpful way** since it gets you an answer, but the answer is not as helpful as it could be. I show this unhelpful way first in the hopes that this will inoculate you against using this method.

*Unhelpful CAC calculation = total spent on marketing in period / number of new customers in period*

That is, to figure out how much it costs a business to bring in one more paying customer, just take the total spent on all customer acquisition activities (ads, meetings, fliers, emails, etc) over a set time, say last month, and then count up all the new customers in that period. Divide the total spend by the number of new customers and that's your CAC...

*If possible, don't do that.*

Yes, many people calculate CAC that way, especially when looking at summary data in an annual report. But unless you need a quick and dirty answer and can accept that it will be misleading, don't do that for your own CAC calculations where you likely have more information.

Here's what's wrong with the above calculation.

In that calculation, we simply take the total spend and divide it by the total number of customers. That means that if people take more time than the period we measure to convert to become a customer (which can be common), then you will count the wrong people. You might be succeeding, not know it, and by changing course make your business worse.

Second, even if timing isn't a problem, the calculation is very rough. Which of the marketing activities led to new customers? We can't tell from the calculation above. In the past, there was an advertising joke often repeated: "I know that I waste half of my advertising dollars. I just don't know which half." The unhelpful calculation keeps the joke going. Today, it's often possible to know which half doesn't work, or at least get a better approximation. What if we were more specific in the way we calculated CAC?

Third, the formula doesn't give us insight on where we can improve. Are we spending too much on marketing? Are we not acquiring enough customers for how much we spend? We can't tell.

# Customer Acquisition Cost Done Better

*Improving the earlier CAC equation.*

Instead of the above, a better way is to calculate CAC by thinking on an individual customer basis. Rather than calculate CAC overall, using all spending on customer acquisition and all new customers gained, we'll break this formula into its individual components. This will give us a more detailed view.

Basic components of CAC that we'll start with are:
- The cost to get a potential customer "in the door,"
- The conversion rate at which a potential customer becomes an actual customer.

Since this book covers both online and offline businesses, I use the "in the door" description. That way, someone who lands on your website or in your brick and mortar location can be counted according to the same formula. There are many examples of what could bring someone "in the door," from online ads, word of mouth, content marketing, influencer marketing, to print, and even billboards.

Of that list, it's most straightforward to calculate the cost to get someone "in the door" for an online ad. Someone sees the ad, clicks it for more information, the business pays for the click, and then has the opportunity to convert the visitor into a customer. Let's look into this.

Let's say that it costs a business $1 every time a viewer clicks on an ad for the business's product. This is a cost that is set by a market operating within Facebook, LinkedIn, Google, or other ad networks that sell ad space. That $1 cost for a click is a function of a few things, such as the customer segment being targeted, competition for the same access, and also the relevance or past performance of that ad to the particular product.

The second part of the equation is the conversion rate of people who are targeted. Conversion rate is the percentage of people who see information about your product (they clicked on your ad) and then convert to buying. So if 100 people see your ad for skateboards or party hats and five of those purchase the product, then you have a conversion rate of 5% for that ad.

This rate will change over time, by type of ad content, by the type of targeted person, by awareness with the product... by a lot of things. Let's plug these numbers into the "Better CAC Calculation" shown below.

## Better CAC Calculation

*CAC = cost to get a potential customer "in the door" / conversion rate to becoming a customer*

*CAC = $1 / 5% = $20*

It's still simple, but an improvement on the previous "Unhelpful CAC Calculation." This better version of the formula helps us more easily break our CAC result into a per customer cost. It also includes two essential metrics that drive CAC. When you define CAC this way you get some insight into what you can improve when you talk to others in business. Do others pay as much as you to bring a potential customer "in the door"? Do others see similar conversion rates? With this simple CAC formula, you can start to evaluate your own performance.

You do still need to track how customers convert, but connecting clicks and future purchases is now a feature of many ad platforms. It's tougher but still possible to track other traditional ways to drive customer acquisition.

# Customer Acquisition Cost By Channel

*What is a channel? Why should we break out CAC by channel?*

A channel is a specific path to a customer. It's the way people learn about your business. There are many examples, including the online ads we mentioned, social media, conferences, print, word of mouth, and many more.

To make the CAC calculation more useful, rather than show a single CAC, we'll break out CAC by channel. That is, we'll calculate CAC as shown in the previous chapter, but rather than in the aggregate, we'll calculate it separately for each customer channel. This provides more insight into what channels currently work and which we might need to tweak or abandon.

### CAC Calculation
*CAC = cost to get a potential customer "in the door" / conversion rate to becoming a customer*

Breaking this out by channel, we might see the following (numbers for demonstration only).

*CAC (of Facebook ads) = $1.50 per click / 3% conversion rate = $50 (40% of acquisitions)*
*CAC (of LinkedIn ads) = $2 per click / 5% conversion rate = $40 (25% of acquisitions)*
*CAC (of social media post) = $0 per post / 6% conversion rate = $0 (35% of acquisitions)*

When thinking about your CAC you can either use the average of all channels or the per channel CACs. But how helpful is an average?

If you take the above and then show a breakdown of your current customer acquisition, you have something like this chart.

CAC of Channel 1: $50
40% of total acquisitions

CAC of Channel 2: $40
25% of total acquisitions

CAC of Channel 3: $0
35% of total acquisitions

## CAC (average = $30)

Let's add a salesperson to the mix.

*CAC (of Facebook ads) = $1.50 per click / 3% conversion rate = $50 (40% of acquisitions)*
*CAC (of LinkedIn ads) = $2 per click / 5% conversion rate = $40 (20% of acquisitions)*
*CAC (of social media post) = $0 per post / 6% conversion rate = $0 (30% of acquisitions)*
*CAC (of salesperson) = $100 per meeting / 12% conversion rate = $833 (10% of acquisitions)*

CAC of Channel 1: $50
40% of total acquisitions

CAC of Channel 2: $40
20% of total acquisitions

CAC of Channel 3: $0
30% of total acquisitions

**CAC
(average =
$110)**

CAC of Channel 4: $833
10% of total acquisitions

Now for the four channels above your average CAC is around $110. But how helpful is that average? And is a higher CAC worse?

It's important to break out CAC by channel because some channels will work longer than others. For example, if you keep buying Facebook ads, your cost per click will probably eventually increase and your conversion rate will probably eventually decrease. You'll saturate your targeted market with the ads and only the potential customers who are less likely to convert will be left. That will drive up the CAC of that channel.

While we know which channels are cheaper, we still don't know which are better. Or even what "better" means yet. We can't simply choose the lowest cost channel since we don't yet have pieces of the overall puzzle, such as LTV per channel and payback period. That's why we can't really say if the above salesperson is cheap and worth it or expensive and not worth it.

It is expected that your CAC will be different by channel. After all, each channel has different costs associated with it and different potential customers who will convert at different rates. And often, along the way, the CAC will change. Regardless of change in CAC, some channels can grow quickly and some cannot.

# Conversion Funnels

*What's a conversion funnel? How does it represent our efforts to acquire customers and the way we can calculate CAC?*

A conversion funnel is a representation of the way potential customers gain awareness of your product, how they then sign up, start to pay, generate referrals, and more.

Here's a common representation, with sample percentage losses at each stage of the funnel. To read this, think of new potential customers becoming aware of your business and then flowing down the funnel. By the end of the funnel, only some are left.

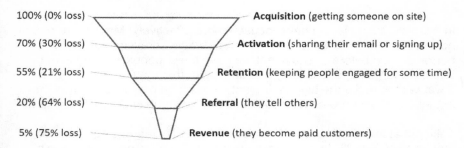

I show the percentage remaining at each stage of the funnel, plus the loss from the previous stage (in parenthesis). That's the loss from the previous stage, so going from 70% to 55% is a loss of 21%. That's (70% - 55%) / 70% = 21% (and not 15%). I do the calculation that way so I can focus on the parts of the funnel where the loss is the greatest.

I'll simplify this funnel to just look at a few stages. Here's another example.

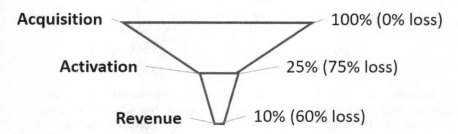

In this example, we may be casting too wide of a net and wasting time on people who are not our target segment.

If we want to make the biggest impact focusing on one single part of the funnel, the most drop-off comes in the Activation stage (75% loss). Say we do that and now the conversions look like this.

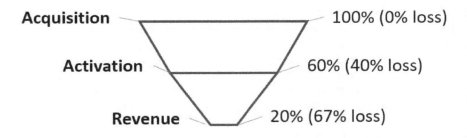

**Acquisition** — 100% (0% loss)

**Activation** — 60% (40% loss)

**Revenue** — 20% (67% loss)

In this next example, we have focused more effectively. Many more people now activate and more result in revenue as well. I drew the funnel narrower than before to show that we have fewer people coming in at the top. If we targeting a smaller group of people, that may be good or bad. If we want to make the biggest impact focusing on one single part of the funnel, the most drop-off now comes in the Revenue stage (67% loss).

Taking that improvement, we now focus on the Revenue stage and get that up to 40% (33% loss from previous stage). I have again drawn this next new funnel as narrower than before to show that we have fewer people coming in at the top.

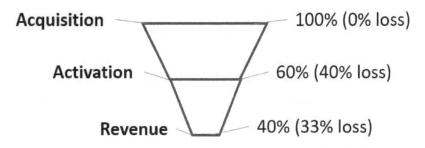

**Acquisition** — 100% (0% loss)

**Activation** — 60% (40% loss)

**Revenue** — 40% (33% loss)

In this example, many more people entering the funnel end up becoming paying customers. What we don't know from a conversion funnel is how that changes the total number of people we can potentially work with. If improving the funnel in this way means that we potentially have many fewer customers overall, we may make less revenue. We may also spend less on customer acquisition.

What does this mean for our CAC and later LTV? Let's bring some more numbers in.

If we do a paid ad campaign on the first three-part simplified funnel that costs us $1 per click, then those people entering at the top of the funnel cost us $1 each. That's before we know how well they will convert to paid customers. Let's say that we can get 1,000 people to the top of the funnel with this campaign.

The Activation phase costs us nothing extra (assuming we're not giving anything else away and maintaining them on site is without costs).

But only 10% become paid customers. That gives us CAC of $1 / 10% = $10.

Our product is priced at $10/month, with costs of $5/month. So contribution margin is $5/month. We breakeven on a paid customer after month 2. (I'm leaving out retention to keep this example simple.)

Total number of paid customers = 1,000 x 10% = 100. Total spent on campaign = $1,000. Total earned after 5 months (assuming no churn to keep it simple) = $5/month x 5 months x 100 = $2,500. That's a 1 : 2.5 ratio of spending to earning and a total $1,500 difference.

Let's now look at the last conversion funnel above. In this example, we'll target more narrowly. Let's say that we can only get 100 people to the top of the funnel with this campaign.

I'll keep the ad campaign at the same cost (this would realistically probably change) of $1 per click, so that those people entering at the top of the funnel still cost us $1 each. That's before we know how well they will convert to paid customers.

The Activation phase again costs us nothing extra.

But now 40% become paid customers. That gives us CAC of $1 / 40% = $2.50.

Our product is still priced at $10/month, with costs of $5/month. So contribution margin is $5/month. And now we breakeven on a paid customer halfway through month 1.

But those 100 people at the top of the funnel only gain us 40 new customers. We spent less but also earn less.

Total number of paid customers = 100 x 40% = 40. Total spent on campaign = $100. Total earned after 5 months (assuming no churn to keep it simple) = $5/month x 5 months x 40 = $1,000. That's a better 1 : 10 ratio of spending to earning, but a smaller total $900 difference.

# Growing and Scaling Customer Acquisition

*What's the difference between growing and scaling? Does customer acquisition grow or scale across all channels? How does CAC change over time?*

When something increases in size we can say that it grows. But when something increases in size and also becomes more efficient, we can say that it scales.

Businesses that don't scale have variable costs that rise in line (or more) with their growth. Businesses that do scale use their fixed costs as a way to serve more customers without a similar increase in variable costs.

There are also businesses that are large, but where costs grow more or less linearly or faster. Examples of businesses like this include organizations that provide human-powered consulting, accounting, financial advising, legal, and other services. For an existing large consulting business to sell an additional 10 projects, they would need more consultants, support staff, and equipment. For a scalable business to serve another 1,000 customers with their products they might not need to hire any more staff (although they might need to add equipment or pay for more hosting).

For example, Instagram had tens of millions of downloads and users but only 13 team members when it was acquired by Facebook. This is why there can be business models that support companies with large groups of unpaid users and a small number of paid customers. The cost to acquire and serve these users and customers is low, the business can grow to serve large numbers of them, and therefore (in the case of Instagram) an ad-supported business model can work.

Scalability is a sign that the business becomes more efficient per customer as it grows. For example, if a business adds customers or revenue but its per customer cost declines as it does so. Or, additionally if revenue scales per customer as well.

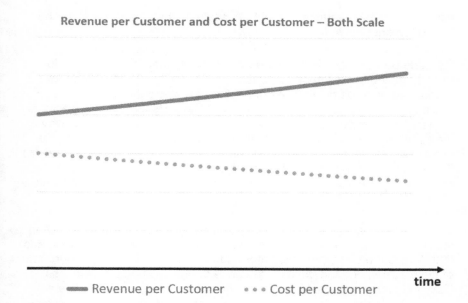

Revenue per Customer and Cost per Customer – Both Scale

Revenue per Customer ••• Cost per Customer

**time**

Growth that is non-scalable is different. There may be an increase in the size of the business, number of customers, revenue, or related metrics. But as this non-scalable business grows the cost per customer does not decline. This could still be a good business, but it is non-scalable. The cost or revenue lines above would stay flat or worsen over time.

Scaling is a common term that deals with how things change as a business moves from being "small" to "large," with efficiencies along the way. This is a point that gets a lot of attention in the media. That doesn't mean that it's focused attention. The idea behind scaling is confusing for a couple reasons.

Scalable businesses are not common. They might be the ones whose logos you recognize. But they are relatively rare. Just in the US, the number of businesses that I'll estimate as scaled (harder to also count the ones that are scalable, but not yet operating as such) would probably be measured in the thousands. I'm making that rough estimate from assuming that many of the startups that raise money show signs of being scalable (whether or not they succeed). And before you say that "thousands" is actually a lot, remember that there are 28 million businesses in the US, almost all of which are small businesses, according to the Small Business Administration. The scalable business number is difficult to estimate since most of the companies are private and don't report many numbers publicly. A simple count of startups doesn't work either since while startups "should" be scalable they aren't always. And they often shut down too.

Scalable businesses often have network effects that make it easier for them to maintain customer acquisition and retention. There are a few reasons for this. As businesses grow, their greater public awareness makes it easier for them to gain new customers. People have already heard of the company and don't need as much education to know why they should become a customer. As a happy customer base grows, the business benefits from existing customer referrals (low or no cost growth) that lead to new customers. There are also funding, cash flow, market power, and other reasons behind why a scalable company can continue to grow.

There are also reasons that growing or scaling companies may experience increased CAC. If the company depends on paid acquisition (running ads), then they often push their customer acquisition cost higher as they run out of ideal customers and drive up the price of advertising to people less likely to convert to a paid customer. The market for space on online ad networks will often drive up the price to display ads that generate lower conversion rates (a demonstration of lower quality). That drives up CAC, per the formula above, on both inputs of the calculation: higher cost to get someone "in the door" and also a lower conversion rate.

Relying on paid acquisition can be dangerous. Companies sometimes get forced into that direction by investor pressure for growth on an accelerated timeline or because they have not invested enough in building customer retention and customer referrals.

Speeding up the activities that grow a customer base is different than scaling a business. As businesses scale, they become more efficient. Their fixed investments can serve a larger number of customers and their per customer variable costs may decrease per customer or per dollar of revenue.

As your business matures and it becomes more important to understand your CAC, how should you look at this metric, and what enables you to grow or scale?

# Are Customer Acquisition Costs Variable or Fixed?

*Why it's confusing to calculate some CACs.*

The way we've discussed calculating CAC relies on a direct connection between a product and a potential customer, knowing the cost of each interaction, and the likelihood of conversion to paid (potential customers become actual customers).

What about when we don't know these inputs because the path to a customer is less direct? After all, not knowing these inputs is the normal state of affairs. It's only in recent times that we have been able to track each step of the path to a customer. Here's a common example.

You spend 10 hours to create a creative asset, like a blog post, video, or case study. You can value the time spent in that creation at an hourly rate that you set for yourself, something people usually find difficult to do. If it's easier, estimate what you would need to pay someone else for that creation.

That creative asset is then discoverable for free. When a visitor searches for something relevant, discovers the asset, pays and becomes a customer, how do you put a number to the CAC?

This fixed asset continues to generate traffic and customers over time. Whether it creates a total of one customer or a stream of thousands a month, the business is not charged more for more conversions. That's the good news. You don't know today, but can estimate what it takes for the creative asset to pay for itself.

Look at how many customers are needed for break even.

*Break even number of customers = cost of asset creation /* contribution margin *of one additional customer*

# Scaling Customer Acquisition Channels

*Noting differences in channels and ways to grow.*

When the time is right we can plan to increase spending on customer acquisition. If, for example, our CAC to LTV ratio is "good," then we might decide to spend more on customer acquisition, either in aggregate or on an individual interaction basis.

Managers of growth look for creative opportunities to change the normal outcomes.

Let's look at the following channels. Which ones do you think will grow or scale by supporting more and more customer acquisition activity?

- *Email (from a list already built)*
- *Paid ads on large networks like Facebook, Google, LinkedIn, Twitter, Snapchat*
- *Paid ads on a niche site highly targeted to our audience*
- *Content you write on your business' website*
- *Media coverage*
- *SEO*
- *Content posted to online forums*
- *Social media posts*
- *Print ads*
- *Word of Mouth (WOM)*
- *Referrals from customers*

Here is what I think you'll find.

**Email (from a list already built)**. Growing a mailing list takes time. People need to discover your business' content, sign up for it, and continue to read it. You can impact how this channel scales by both growing the list (getting access to more people and providing value that makes them sign up), sending emails more frequently (more of a chance that your subscribers will see the emails), and also making your emails better at converting readers to customers (split-testing). When you build a large email list, continual testing becomes essential. One company, CB Insights, sends test variations of its daily email to a small percent of its audience and evaluates results in the first hour before deciding on a winning subject line. It then uses the winning subject line for the rest of the day. In their case, they estimated a significant rise in sales just because of that practice.

*It can grow, but requires investment and testing to scale.*

**Paid ads on large networks like Facebook, Google, LinkedIn, Twitter, Snapchat**. In general, your CAC on a paid channel may look like this.

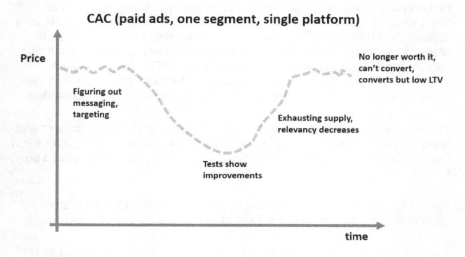

**CAC (paid ads, one segment, single platform)**

At the start when you are figuring out what content works, what images and copy are attractive, and what users to target, your CAC may be on the high side. Then eventually you start to make improvements and CAC falls. Then, as you continue to spend, CAC starts to rise again. You have already marketed to the most attractive customer segments who want your product the most. Everyone who was going to convert has converted to a customer. Your ad's relevancy score (Facebook term) falls (a mark of how much users like the ad content), conversion rates drop, and CAC rises. Additionally, outside of your control, a platform algorithm change can unexpectedly disrupt how well your ad buys work. If CAC rises far enough, you might just discontinue your ad spend altogether.

*It can grow acquisitions (you can just keep buying ads), but it will become more expensive and so it doesn't scale.*

**Paid ads on a niche site highly targeted to your audience**. For a niche site you may be able expect a higher conversion rate since the audience is more targeted. Then again, larger networks usually offer the ability to target groups of users with a lot of specificity.

*It can grow acquisitions (you can just keep buying ads), but it will become more expensive and so it doesn't scale. You might find a higher conversion rate because the audience is more targeted.*

**Content you produce for your business' website**. Staying focused on CAC and direct business models, let's think of website content as serving the purpose of converting readers to paid customers. If you produce with that purpose, then we judge content by its ability to bring people in and turn them into customers. What activities make website content scale as a channel and how does CAC change? First, we could focus our effort to produce content in areas that are already interesting to a large group of people, for example by looking at search trends. That helps us get a volume of visitors who are already searching for our information. We then focus on accessing and converting a higher percentage of those readers.

This channel is different in that the cost for you to develop the content and bring people "in the door" is probably the cost of your own time (unless you pay someone for content development). Either way, you really should put a monetary figure to it.

Since the content can continue to generate customers for a long time, content actually functions like a fixed cost.

*It can both grow acquisitions and scale, but requires long-term investment in content development.*

**Media coverage**. Some businesses gain customers by being noteworthy to journalists. This helps drive down CAC.

*It can both grow acquisitions but not necessarily scale. Requires reaching out to the right journalists at the right time. No guarantee that they will write about the business or what perspective they might take.*

**SEO**. Appearing in search results can drive traffic at low cost. Whether there is a volume of traffic depends on what search terms the business ranks for and how highly it ranks.

*It can both grow acquisitions and scale, but requires long-term investment in content development and SEO optimization.*

**Content posted to online forums**. Similarities to content produced above, except that posts to forums tend to "expire" in relevance after a while.

*It can grow acquisitions but not scale. It requires long-term investment in content development.*

**Social media posts**. Similarities to content produced above, except that social media posts tend to "expire" after a while. Few followers ever see them. I usually see an engagement rate of below 1% of the follower base for typical social media posts.

*It can grow acquisitions and could also scale if you grow followers who share more of your posts. This requires long-term investment in content development.*

**Print ads**. Here again, you can keep buying print ads and can experiment with the ads you run. The print ad (and more specifically direct mail) business has been around for a long time. Many of the split-test techniques were originally run on paper decades ago. At volume, small improvements add up.

*It can grow acquisitions (you can just keep buying ad space), but it will become less useful as you run out of viewers and so it doesn't scale.*

**Word of Mouth (WOM)**. In theory there is no cost when WOM happens naturally. It is sometimes possible, when there is a strong product, to grow purely from customer referrals.

*It can grow acquisitions (people who love your products tell others). It remains free and possible to scale, but it is not necessarily possible to turn on WOM when you want it. You can't force people to talk about you. You can only be remarkable enough to talk about. WOM can become more effective over time as more people spread the word about your business, so it could scale.*

**In general**, the reality that CAC can increase over time can be problematic for growing businesses that are not also able to grow how much they earn from the new customers. It makes sense that early customers can be acquired for less -- those are the people who most need what the business provides. Later customers may take more convincing or may generate less value back to the business (the LTV question, which we'll get to later).

Each of the above channels behaves differently. Some do not scale much at all, some scale while increasing in cost, some take time to scale, and some can scale quickly. It's important to remember that while investing in customer acquisition to grow your business.

Investors often ask questions around the scalability of the current state of your business into the future. How do you acquire customers today and how will that change as you grow? How will the cost of each channel change as you grow?

# Customer Acquisition Cost by Cycle Time

*What is cycle time and why should we care about it?*

Often, or almost always for some business types, your marketing spend does not result in an immediate customer relationship. This means that the formula we've been using above (CAC = cost to get someone "in the door" / conversion rate) can be misleading. Some businesses, often those selling understandable and functional products, or products that are impulse buys, or products that are common purchases at low price points, can convert a customer with minimal time after they hear about the product. But for many other businesses, there is a longer time lag before that conversion. Months or even years can pass before potential customers become actual customers.

In an extreme example, imagine how uncommon it is for a large purchase to be made quickly and as a result of a direct appeal to potential customers. For example, in 2016 when Tesla offered the public the right to pay online to reserve a Model 3, they broke records not for car sales, but for crowdfunding. The potential customers put down $1,000 to reserve a car, not to buy it outright. There was no fixed timeline for car delivery and people could still decide not to buy.

Keeping with the luxury car example, car brands spend years spreading their marketing across various channels before their conversion of a new customer who has seen the messaging. The beginning of luxury car marketing may be to people too young to drive.

You can mitigate long cycle times by extending your product line. In the luxury car example above it seems natural that a potential customer would only rarely convert to become an actual customer. Luxury cars are, for most people, rare or impossible purchases. That means that acquiring a customer takes a long time (and many never convert). But what if there were other ways -- beyond the luxury car -- for people to be customers? The car business could extend its product line in several directions.

For Ferrari, cars, spare parts, and engines account for around 80% of revenues. But beyond cars, Ferrari sells and licenses bikes, watches, pens, eyeglasses, apparel, theme parks, Formula 1, and sponsorships. Together, those produce over 15% of revenue. Ferrari can have customers at many different price points and most without ever sitting in a car. And some non-customers will convert years later.

Similar to the earlier formula, this one provides the number of periods needed until you break even on the CAC. If you have a CAC of $50 but people spend $0 for the first seven months and then generate $10/month in gross margin after that, then in one year you break even on their acquisition.

*Time to break even = CAC / time until total customer* contribution margin *equals CAC*

# What Should My CAC Be?

*How does a business know what CAC it might expect? Is simply minimizing CAC the goal? When should you seek higher CAC?*

Since there are multiple variables in calculating CAC, you can benchmark against others in a similar industry or those who sell to similar customer segments, but your results may be different.

Research results across multiple industries. These results might be different than what you experience because of the way you target your ads, your design, and your products.

Economic changes can impact CAC. For example, after years of cost per click increases, COVID-19 brought uncertainty to a number of businesses which in turn led to a drop in ad spending and ad platform cost per click. This drop in costs was advantageous for some businesses.

To get a better perspective you might also talk with people who see a lot of different companies (if they can share their perspective).

Looking at single, static numbers for LTV, or for payback periods such as Months to Recover CAC, can produce misleading numbers.

Few metrics should be taken in isolation. Change one and you often change others. Similarly, with CAC, the goal cannot simply be to minimize CAC. If higher CACs also drive higher LTVs, then you may be better off spending more to acquire customers. If higher CACs result in shorter payback cycle times, then you may want to seek out these increased CACs. If you are after market share, then accepting higher CACs may be worth it.


# Customer Acquisition Cost Summary

Remember that our goals here were to make our customer acquisition model:
- Specific, by understanding differences by each channel,
- Predictive, by understanding how costs and conversions change over time and whether these activities can grow or scale,
- Fit with the business model (more on that below in the LTV section).

# Lifetime Value (LTV)

## Introduction

Lifetime Value is a measure of contribution margin a business earns from selling to a customer over time. We often talk about LTV as a prediction of what customers will do. It is often only businesses that have been around for a while that have enough data to accurately predict customer behavior.

While LTV is incredibly important, it can also be highly problematic as a metric. Unlike CAC, which can be measured up front, LTV is different.

LTV is made up of unit price, unit cost, and customer repeat purchases. Other factors like cycle time also come into consideration.

LTV can also mislead because you will often see it calculated in multiple ways while the name remains the same. As earlier with CAC, I'm going to show the common, unhelpful calculations first, so that you can recognize them and see why they are not helpful.

Also, LTV is usually presented as a single number: what I call static LTV. You can think of LTV that way – many people do -- but I also want you to recognize that LTV as a static number is misleading and even harmful (we'll explore why).

# Lifetime Value an Unhelpful Way (A Way You Often See It)

*How do you often see LTV calculated? Why is this problematic?*

Gray's Papaya is an iconic hot dog restaurant (it's true) in Manhattan, NYC. Since 1985 they have had a meal called the "Recession Special" (also true), which is a medium drink and two hotdogs. When I was much younger I used to eat the Recession Special standing at their counter, followed by a papaya drink.

I remember when the Recession Special was $1.95 but the price has gone up since then.

Let's calculate LTV in the **common unhelpful way** that many people use. Warning: *This is for inoculating you against doing this in the future. Do not really use this calculation in your work! Also, restaurants are more concerned with throughput or revenue per square foot rather than individual customer retention, so this is just to work through an example...*

*Unhelpful LTV calculation = Price of the product X Number of times the customer buys*

Let's assume that everyone only buys the Recession Special and that they buy it 10 times (which was probably what I did). That means that the common, but unhelpful LTV for Gray's Papaya is:

*Unhelpful LTV = Price X Number of times an individual customer buys it = $1.95 X 10 = $19.95*

If a customer keeps buying, they are retained. Therefore, Gray's Papaya earned $19.95 from me over the course of my time as a customer with them. Maybe I moved away from NYC (true). Maybe I just couldn't eat more (also true).

*Now let's look at why the above calculation is misleading.*

Solely using price without considering margin will give you misleading LTV numbers. Here's an example that is actually pretty common.

In the unhelpful LTV calculation, we have Price and Number of times Purchased. That means that if I can improve on either of those components I've improved my LTV.

So if I keep the price at $1.95 but double purchases from 10 to 20 ($1.95 X 20 = $39, which is double $19.95) or if I can double the price to $3.90 and still keep people for 10 purchases ($3.90 X 10 = $39), I have the same effect on the business, right?

That's what people assume, but that's also why this incorrect LTV calculation is problematic. One reason is, in this LTV calculation we don't know how much it costs to provide the product to our customers.

For example, if the cost of ingredients to Gray's Papaya is $0.50 and they charge $1.95 across 10 servings, then their contribution margin is $1.45 per meal. Multiplied by the 10 times I visit, it's $1.45 X 10 = $14.50. When we doubled the number of repeat purchases to 20, Gray's then earns $1.45 X 20 = $29.

But in the second example we kept the number of purchases the same but doubled the price to $3.90. That means that since the cost of the meal is still $0.50, Gray's would make $3.40 X 10 = $34.

Two different LTVs. That's why this common form of LTV is misleading.

# Lifetime Value Done Better

The first improvement we made to the above LTV calculation was to add in the cost of producing the product or of providing the service. Here's the better calculation:

*LTV = (Price of product – Cost to produce) X Number of times the customer buys*

This LTV calculation adds in the costs that the first calculation left out. Price per unit – Cost per unit gives us the Contribution Margin.

When you calculate LTV, keep all three of these inputs separate. Do not simplify the formula to be your Contribution Margin X Number of times the customer buys. To show you why, think about this example.

*Price = $98*
*Cost to produce = $97*
*Number of purchases across time = 10*
*That means that LTV = ($98 - $97) X 10 = $10*

If we track numbers, whether LTV, CAC or other metrics, they give us insight on where we might improve our business. So if we simplified the above example to be LTV = Contribution Margin X Repeat Purchases = $1 X 10 = $10, then we lose a lot of information. We don't know if there is an opportunity to benefit from a changed price or improved costs.

In the above example, to double LTV, we could increase our price about 1% from $98 to $99, reduce unit cost to $96, or we could double retention to 20 purchases. If it's more likely to be able to increase the price or reduce cost than double repeat purchases, we lose that insight if we simplify the formula to only include contribution margin. In the above example it's probably easier to double contribution margin than purchases.

The Recession Special today is $6.95. If you update the above numbers so that price increases over time and costs increase over time, you also get a better sense of LTV.

Estimated Cost of Goods Sold (COGS) of the Gray's Papaya Recession Special = sum of the estimated wholesale price of two Sabrett's hot dogs ($0.55), two hotdog buns ($0.10), added ketchup ($0.01), mustard ($0.01), relish ($0.01) and fried onions ($0.01), the two small paper plates to hold the hot dogs ($0.01), the cost of the drink ($0.25), the paper cup ($0.01), plastic cup top ($0.02), straw ($0.01), and napkin ($0.01), = $1.00 (estimate).

*Note: I am still not an expert in running a hot dog business. The above is my estimate. I have not spoken to anyone at Gray's Papaya although I am open to a lunchtime meeting the next time I'm in New York.*

What happens if price changes over time along with changes in cost? How does that change our LTV calculation? This is why calculating LTV in the static way above only tells part of the story.

**Updated LTV calculation**
LTV of Gray's Papaya Customer = (Price – COGS) X Number of times Customer buys = ($6.95 - $1.00) X 10 = $59.50.

Done, right? No.

The static single number LTV calculation is misleading because it also leaves out timing. Even if you avoid the common mistakes made above, timing is where you'll have trouble. We track LTV for several reasons, including knowing how fast we can grow and how much we should pay to acquire a customer.

What would happen if we factored in a changing price? How long it took the price to change? When the customer makes their purchases? Changes in margin? Addition of new products? Here's a demonstration of what you could do.

| Customer Purchase | 1 | 3 | 4 | 5 | 6 | 7 | 8 | 9 | 10 |
|---|---|---|---|---|---|---|---|---|---|
| Price | 1.95 | 1.95 | 2.95 | 2.95 | 4.95 | 5.95 | 5.95 | 6.95 | 6.95 |
| Costs | -0.50 | -0.60 | -0.70 | -0.70 | -0.80 | -0.90 | -1.00 | -1.00 | -1.00 |
| Contribution Margin | 1.45 | 1.35 | 2.25 | 2.25 | 4.15 | 5.05 | 4.95 | 5.95 | 5.95 |
| Cumulative | 1.45 | 4.25 | 6.50 | 8.75 | 12.90 | 17.95 | 22.90 | 28.85 | 34.80 |

There are many ways to produce better estimates of LTV.

# Lifetime Value Done Even Better

Let's dive into each of the components of LTV to see what they are, how we can adjust them, and how they relate to each other.

**Price**

Price is many things. Price can be a mark of quality, a way to adjust customer behavior, a reflection of costs, a measure of value, an attempt to fit into a set of other options customers have...

Price per unit is not necessarily the same for every customer. Price can be dynamic, as with surge pricing on Uber or Lyft. It can be fixed, as on printed restaurant menus. Price can be related to variations in what customers receive, as with basic and premium versions of the same product. Price can change based on who is the customer, where they are located, what qualities of the product they use, when they use it, how much, and more.

Price can also be based on behavior and signals. In 2015 Apple launched its line of Apple watches. Apple manages new product releases very well, but its watches gained public attention for different reasons than normal. When Apple introduced its watches there were three rough pricing categories. There was the "inexpensive" watch at $349 and a luxury version, with the casing milled from gold (but otherwise the same watch), at $20,000. A lot of press wrote about the $20,000 watch, which only served to spread the word about the "affordable" $349 version. That's a channel CAC of $0 to sell a product with a contribution margin estimated at $90 in the cheap version.

As others have suggested, the purpose of the $20,000 gold watch was both to serve the small niche that actually wanted those products but certainly also to draw attention to the cheaper options.

**Cost**

Cost represents the sum of inputs needed to produce a unit of the product for a customer. Whether we produce a physical item like a cup of coffee, or a digital one like cloud hosting, there are costs. Sometimes the costs are more easily conceptualized, like in the coffee. Sometimes the costs are more complicated and based on usage and other factors, as in hosting. For that reason, for many of my early examples I use physical products.

What I don't include here are the other fixed costs associated with running the business. Things like rent, staffing, insurance, utilities, and more unless these can be directly associated with the delivery of one unit of a product to a customer. These other costs tend not to move in line with sales. That is, in most cases, a business' rent, staff, or utilities costs stay the same if you make another sale, both because it can serve more customers without disturbing the existing setup and also because businesses tend to add those costs in chunks rather than constantly readjusting for every new sale.

## Retention

Retention is a helpful metric to track repeat purchases and engagement. I forced the retention metric in the Gray's Papaya example above. Restaurants are not typically businesses with predictable purchases from the same individuals. Restaurant customers don't agree to visit monthly or to buy a set amount of food monthly.

Businesses that have long-term user retention and relatively unchanging products can sometimes measure retention accurately. For example, mobile phone operators can often calculate user retention to fractions of a percentage point. This brings a high degree of predictability to their businesses. You can calculate retention on any time period that makes sense.

Remember that if someone doesn't pay, they aren't a customer. That means that for a social network like Facebook, the 2.5 billion people they have (who don't pay) are called "users" and their customers are the 7 million advertisers who pay to reach these users. In the first couple years, Facebook operated without advertising. It had no customers back then. But today Facebook generates revenues of over $80 billion per year. But since users are the reason advertising customers want to be on Facebook, key metrics for the company and other social networks are retention related, such as daily active users (DAU).

# LTV Is a River

*Why is LTV not just a single number? Why is considering LTV a series of flows (like a river) a better description of what's happening?*

The problem I have with the static measure of LTV is that while it does simplify the metric to a single number, that number is always going to be misleading. It's more helpful to think of LTV as a flow of inputs and outputs. Like a river.

Sometimes the LTV river flows smoothly. Sometimes it's rapids. Sometimes it loses more water from evaporation than it gains from precipitation. Sometimes it stops flowing until the winter snows melt in the spring. Sometimes there is just one single river the whole way and sometimes many small rivulets combine to form one large river. Keeping with the river analogy, you can't water the crops of your business today with water that will flow tomorrow. Understanding timing is essential with LTV. That's why the single static number version of LTV is a problem.

An easy way to look at LTV as a river is to chart it out on a spreadsheet.

Below is a simple example. The assumption in the model is that customers start with a product's limited free version, upgrade, and then are charged monthly while churning away. Churn is kept constant at an additional 5% a month and not compounded. Take a look.

| Period | 0 | 1 | 2 | 3 | 4 | 5 | 6 | 7 | 8 | 9 | 10 | 11 | 12 |
|---|---|---|---|---|---|---|---|---|---|---|---|---|---|
| CAC | -15.00 | | | | | | | | | | | | |
| Revenue per customer | | 0.00 | 0.00 | 0.00 | 0.00 | 0.00 | 25.00 | 25.00 | 25.00 | 25.00 | 25.00 | 25.00 | 25.00 |
| Costs per customer | | -5.00 | -5.00 | -5.00 | -5.00 | -5.00 | -10.00 | -10.00 | -10.00 | -10.00 | -10.00 | -10.00 | -10.00 |
| Gross profit per customer | | -5.00 | -5.00 | -5.00 | -5.00 | -5.00 | 15.00 | 15.00 | 15.00 | 15.00 | 15.00 | 15.00 | 15.00 |
| Retained in period | | 100% | 95% | 90% | 85% | 80% | 75% | 70% | 65% | 60% | 55% | 50% | 45% |
| Weighted customer gross profit | | -5.00 | -4.75 | -4.50 | -4.25 | -4.00 | 11.25 | 10.50 | 9.75 | 9.00 | 8.25 | 7.50 | 6.75 |
| Cumulative | | -5.00 | -9.75 | -14.25 | -18.50 | -22.50 | -11.25 | -0.75 | 9.00 | 18.00 | 26.25 | 33.75 | 40.50 |

This shows when flows come in, when we breakeven, and what modifications could improve the situation. A single static LTV number doesn't help as much.

# LTV With Cohorts

Just as we split CAC into different channels, we can do something similar with LTV.

Retention is an important part of LTV that shows the loss of customers over time. Here's a chart showing customers by the month they joined and how many are retained in each month afterward. We'll say that since they just signed up, all customers (100%) are counted as retained in the first month. But after that, retention falls.

| Months | 1 | 2 | 3 | 4 | 5 | 6 | 7 | 8 | 9 | 10 | 11 | 12 |
|---|---|---|---|---|---|---|---|---|---|---|---|---|
| January | 100% | 63% | 47% | 33% | 20% | 17% | 15% | 14% | 14% | 13% | 13% | 13% |
| February | | 100% | 65% | 55% | 51% | 44% | 42% | 39% | 35% | 31% | 30% | 29% |
| March | | | 100% | 65% | 63% | 60% | 59% | 56% | 54% | 50% | 49% | 47% |
| April | | | | 100% | 81% | 77% | 73% | 73% | 72% | 70% | 70% | 68% |
| May | | | | | 100% | 83% | 79% | 77% | 76% | 74% | 73% | 72% |
| June | | | | | | 100% | 87% | 83% | 81% | 79% | 78% | 76% |

To more easily see if the situation is getting better or worse, we rearrange the above chart like the one below. This allows us to more easily compare customers based on when they joined. That is, we want to compare what percent of customers are still paying us in their 6th month. In this chart, LTV has been improving (based on retaining higher percentages of customers in later months).

| Months | 1 | 2 | 3 | 4 | 5 | 6 | 7 | 8 | 9 | 10 | 11 | 12 |
|---|---|---|---|---|---|---|---|---|---|---|---|---|
| January | 100% | 63% | 47% | 33% | 20% | 17% | 15% | 14% | 14% | 13% | 13% | 13% |
| February | 100% | 65% | 55% | 51% | 44% | 42% | 39% | 35% | 31% | 30% | 29% | |
| March | 100% | 65% | 63% | 60% | 59% | 56% | 54% | 50% | 49% | 47% | | |
| April | 100% | 81% | 77% | 73% | 73% | 72% | 70% | 70% | 68% | | | |
| May | 100% | 83% | 79% | 77% | 76% | 74% | 73% | 72% | | | | |
| June | 100% | 87% | 83% | 81% | 79% | 78% | 76% | | | | | |

Graphing the six cohorts above gives us this chart.

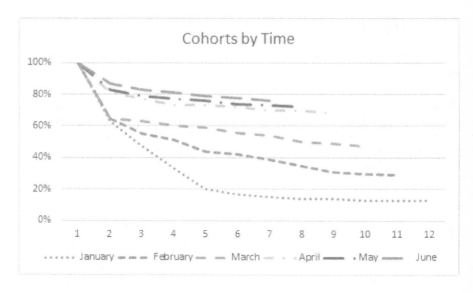

Another way to show cohorts is to group them by customer or user type. Here is an example where we've split out users of a free service (generating revenue from advertising CPM) and customers of the premium service (paying each month). They have different CACs, retention rates, and gross margins, and their break even points come in different months.

| Period | 0 | 1 | 2 | 3 | 4 | 5 | 6 | 7 | 8 | 9 | 10 | 11 | 12 |
|---|---|---|---|---|---|---|---|---|---|---|---|---|---|
| CAC (Free Service) | -10.00 | | | | | | | | | | | | |
| Revenue per customer | | 2.00 | 2.00 | 2.00 | 2.00 | 2.00 | 2.00 | 2.00 | 2.00 | 2.00 | 2.00 | 2.00 | 2.00 |
| Costs per customer | | -0.50 | -0.50 | -0.50 | -0.50 | -0.50 | -0.50 | -0.50 | -0.50 | -0.50 | -0.50 | -0.50 | -0.50 |
| Gross profit per customer | | 1.50 | 1.50 | 1.50 | 1.50 | 1.50 | 1.50 | 1.50 | 1.50 | 1.50 | 1.50 | 1.50 | 1.50 |
| Retention rate in period | 95% | 100% | 95% | 95% | 95% | 95% | 95% | 95% | 95% | 95% | 95% | 95% | 95% |
| Compounded retention rate | | 100% | 95% | 90% | 86% | 81% | 77% | 74% | 70% | 66% | 63% | 60% | 57% |
| Weighted customer gross profit | | 1.50 | 1.43 | 1.35 | 1.29 | 1.22 | 1.16 | 1.10 | 1.05 | 1.00 | 0.95 | 0.90 | 0.85 |
| Cumulative Gross Profit | | 1.50 | 2.93 | 4.28 | 5.56 | 6.79 | 7.95 | 9.05 | 10.10 | 11.09 | 12.04 | 12.94 | 13.79 |
| CAC (Premium) | -50.00 | | | | | | | | | | | | |
| Revenue per customer | | 15.00 | 15.00 | 15.00 | 15.00 | 15.00 | 15.00 | 15.00 | 15.00 | 15.00 | 15.00 | 15.00 | 15.00 |
| Costs per customer | | -5.00 | -5.00 | -5.00 | -5.00 | -5.00 | -5.00 | -5.00 | -5.00 | -5.00 | -5.00 | -5.00 | -5.00 |
| Gross profit per customer | | 10.00 | 10.00 | 10.00 | 10.00 | 10.00 | 10.00 | 10.00 | 10.00 | 10.00 | 10.00 | 10.00 | 10.00 |
| Retention rate in period | 90% | 100% | 90% | 90% | 90% | 90% | 90% | 90% | 90% | 90% | 90% | 90% | 90% |
| Compounded retention rate | | 100% | 90% | 81% | 73% | 66% | 59% | 53% | 48% | 43% | 39% | 35% | 31% |
| Weighted customer gross profit | | 10.00 | 9.00 | 8.10 | 7.29 | 6.56 | 5.90 | 5.31 | 4.78 | 4.30 | 3.87 | 3.49 | 3.14 |
| Cumulative Gross Profit | | 10.00 | 19.00 | 27.10 | 34.39 | 40.95 | 46.86 | 52.17 | 56.95 | 61.26 | 65.13 | 68.62 | 71.76 |

Graphing the cumulative contribution margin of the two cohorts above gives us this chart.

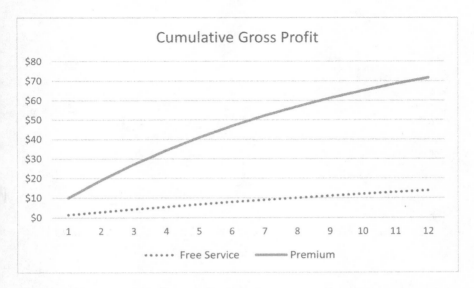

**Cumulative Gross Profit**

Legend: Free Service, Premium

Another way to track customer cohorts is by the way they pay. Let's look at a subscription service that has paid monthly and annual options, as is common.

Payment processing also makes a difference on business decisions. For example, a standard plan from Stripe charges 2.9% plus $0.30 per charge. On a $100/year subscription that is $3.20 ($2.90 + $0.30). But on 12 monthly $10 payments, that turns out to be $7.08 (($0.29 + $0.30) x 12). After payment processing fees, the $100 annual subscription generates $96.80 while the $10 monthly plan turns $120 into $112.91.

In the graph below I show cumulative contribution margin for monthly and annual cohorts over four years. The difference between them comes from payment fees and a monthly 5% churn for the monthly cohort and an annual 30% churn for the annual cohort. Note that while the payment processing fees used are pretty standard, you will find different churn rates depending on business. My only decision on the rates to use came from the normal higher retention of annual customers compared to monthly ones. The difference is more extreme if you add in discounting.

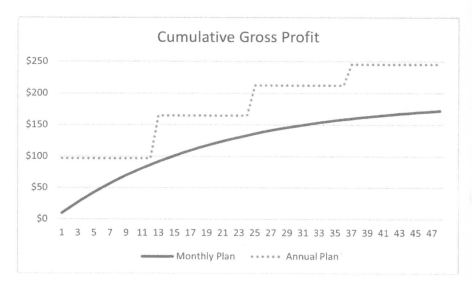

Tracking LTV by cohort can also help you predict what revenue or gross profit flows to expect. Here's an example I made based on several SaaS business cohort analyses. The numbers 1 to 5 at the bottom of the bars in the chart are years. The cohorts 1 to 5, shown in different patterns, track customers that joined in different years. You'll notice that in the early years, the cohorts show declining revenue or gross profit (perhaps the service wasn't as good or they were the wrong customers) but later cohorts show growth over time (they have negative churn).

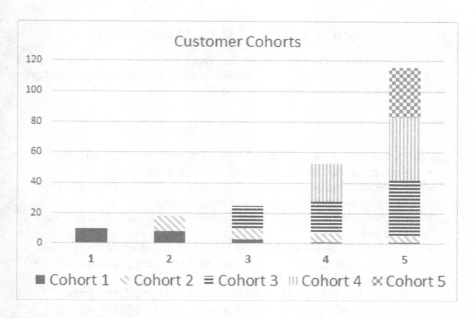

You should track and graph the metrics that matter for your business.
These are just some of the ways.

# Other Reasons Why LTV Is Misleading

Say you have a good handle on LTV for your customers. Your business is at the point where you have predictability in customer spending, retention, and unit costs. What else is there to know?

Lots.

Here are some of the things that LTV calculations still don't help you do:
- Predict future changes to price, cost, and retention.
- Predict entrance of new competition that challenges your model. Competition may affect your prices or costs.
- Predict whether an individual customer will be retained or when they will churn.
- Predict whether churned customers will one day return.
- Predict what customers you can upsell on new products that you haven't yet developed.
- Predict future business decisions that may prioritize market growth, leading you to accept a lower LTV to CAC ratio.

# About CAC to LTV Ratios

*What guidelines are there for ratios between CAC and LTV? Why should there be guidelines at all? When should we use or ignore these guidelines? What examples are there of companies abandoning these guidelines?*

I earlier mentioned the rule of thumb ratio for CAC : LTV of being 1 : 3 or 1 : 4. This is a ratio that you will hear across many industries.

Why does this rule of thumb exist? The 1 : 3 or 1 : 4 ratio is there as a buffer between spending on customer acquisition, all the other costs that come with operating your business that are not CAC, and the risk of generating LTV later on. In other words, you might spend up to one-third of your LTV on acquiring new customers because you need the other two-thirds to continue to operate and cover costs while you wait for the river of LTV to flow in.

The multiple of three to four gives you some breathing room. Apart from the gross profit you earn from purchases in every period that a customer is active, you also have to spend on other costs that are not included in the LTV formula. These include all operating costs, rent, salaries, insurance, tax, travel, hiring, training, and on and on.

The other reason is that it takes time to pay off the CAC. If you work with a multiple like three to four then you probably cover the CAC payback and also give your business room to invest in growth.

So, in general if your CAC to LTV ratio is less favorable than 1 : 3, for example if you only generate $2 for every $1 you spend, you might slow down your investment in growth. If you make more than $4 for every dollar you spend on customer acquisition, you might spend more.

The above ratios are a rule of thumb, not the law. That means that when it makes sense, you should break these rules.

In what situations should you ignore this rule of thumb?

**When you are focused on growing market share.** Early in its history, Amazon had LTV estimates (based on a much smaller product set) and gave employees the right to spend up to the point of LTV in order to acquire customers. That strategy paid off. The company gained market share and as it grew it also added new lines of business, well beyond book sales. That money was well spent. It was also only possible to take that approach by having raised capital and later after educating investors that Amazon intended to delay profitability in order to grow.

**When your payback period makes it difficult.** There are companies that have a good CAC : LTV ratio but where the payback period is too long for them. That is, they can acquire customers cheaply and eventually make back more than the 3x or 4x in LTV the rule of thumb suggests. But for them, earning that LTV takes years. That means that the company can't grow using cash flow from customers. Or in the worst case, by the time the company would make the money back, they are out of business.

**When there are strategic considerations.** Sometimes companies disregard the CAC : LTV ratio because their reality is different. Blue Apron, a meal kit delivery service, has a high CAC and comparably low LTV. That's a terrible situation to be in, except that they kept spending on customer acquisition. The reason? They could. Blue Apron raised $194M and then IPO'd, raising another $300M. Cynically, the spending on customer acquisition is there to provide the opportunity for competitors to fail. It's a strategic decision that can have economic upside. But eventually companies either need to balance their CAC : LTC ratio or go out of business.

# Retention, Churn, and Ways to Calculate Them

*What is retention? What is churn? Why are these metrics important? How are retention or churn misleading?*

Retention is a measure of how many customers or users stay. Churn is a measure of how many customers or users leave. That means that

*Retention = 1 - Churn* and *Churn = 1 - Retention*

To calculate retention, you need a few starting points.

Agreement on what you are measuring retention of. For example, the customer or user of a certain product, a member of a specific cohort, etc.

Agreement on what qualifies as retained or churned. For example, do you need to see monthly activity in users to consider them retained? On what repeated basis do customers need to continue to purchase to be considered retained? Do they need to not renew their annual payment to be considered as churned? Those answers should be determined by the type of business you have.

There are general standards for counting someone as "active." Don't feel that you need to adhere to these standards if they don't fit your situation.

For a subscription service billing monthly (as is typical), retention metrics are typically measured monthly. For other fast-changing and high churn services, such as mobile games, daily or weekly measures are more common.

Once you have agreement on the above, how do you measure retention? A simple way to get started is to look at the past experience with the customers or users you want to measure. When a group of new people become customers, what happens after the first month? What percentage remain as customers?

For example, if you have:
*50 customers at start (month 1), and*
*45 remaining in month two,*
*Retention after one month is then 90%. (45/50)*

With more user information you might be able to make projections. Here are a couple of general ways to do that. Note that these projections might be different from what actually happens.

1. You could assume that you will always lose 5 customers a month:

| Month | 1 | 2 | 3 | 4 | 5 | 6 | 7 | 8 | 9 | 10 | 11 | 12 |
|---|---|---|---|---|---|---|---|---|---|---|---|---|
| Customers | 50 | 45 | 40 | 35 | 30 | 25 | 20 | 15 | 10 | 5 | 0 | 0 |

2. You could assume that you will always lose 10% of the remaining customers each month:

| Month | 1 | 2 | 3 | 4 | 5 | 6 | 7 | 8 | 9 | 10 | 11 | 12 |
|---|---|---|---|---|---|---|---|---|---|---|---|---|
| Customers | 50.0 | 45.0 | 40.5 | 36.5 | 32.8 | 29.5 | 26.6 | 23.9 | 21.5 | 19.4 | 17.4 | 15.7 |

It's not that one is right and the other wrong. It's a question of what describes your customer behavior. I see people use version 1 where it is easy to make estimates (you can immediately say how many periods a customer will stay before churning). I see people use version 2 where they believe that they are always losing a fixed percentage of those remaining – though early churn is probably very different from later churn.

Here's the visual for the two charts above.

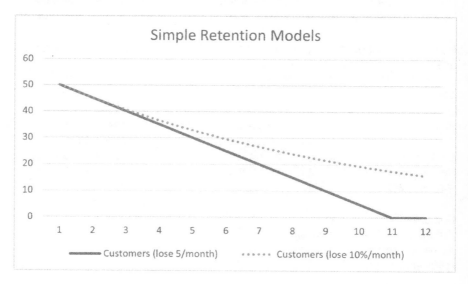

Neither model is useful unless it is good at describing reality. That's why modeling retention is a problem for many early-stage businesses. They don't yet know what the reality is.

# Retention Behaviors

We never have total predictability. There will always be differences in how different companies, with different products and different customers keep them engaged. But as you learn about your customers, observe their behavior, and learn more about how companies with similar products perform, you can probably make some estimates on customer retention.

There are a few retention models I recommend you be aware of.

Tomasz Tunguz, a VC at Redpoint, describes different types of retention curves. Consider what type of retention curve you may be encouraging through the way your business interacts with customers.

**Constant**. Churn is constant month to month. This type is similar to the retention charts shown above.

**Annual**. This type occurs when customers need to make annual decisions to continue as a customer. That could be the requirement to make an annual payment.

**Cliffs**. High churn in the first couple periods and then low churn afterward (everyone who stays is a good fit).

We should derive our models from reality, but we can take some insight from the above examples.

We might find **constant churn** in commodity services that stay the same over time and which also have customer lock-in. For example, mobile phone service providers often see something like a 1% - 3% monthly churn for postpaid service (as opposed to prepaid service, which targets a different segment and has higher churn). These numbers depend on where you are and in general give mobile operators an average customer lifetime of around three to five years. The churn is smooth for a few reasons:

For postpaid mobile phone customers:
- There's no immediate drop-off because people know what they are getting when they sign up. Mobile service is a utility.
- There is little seasonal variance because people use their phones year-round in similar ways. It's not the kind of service where you would use all of your phone service in part of the year so that you can cancel it for the other part of the year.

- There are few dramatic price swings among mobile carriers. The price discount would need to be significant for a customer to put up with the hassle of switching service.
- Number portability, which rolled out in different countries at different times, in general increased churn, but only when price drops or other features rolled out.

At times, mobile operators increased the churn of their competitors, for example by negotiating deals for exclusivity of a highly demanded handset, like AT&T and Telefonica did with the iPhone when it launched in some national markets.

But retention graphs are often not like the ones experienced by mobile operators and utility apps. Unlike mobile phone services after number portability, data storage services increase in value as you increase usage and time on service. The longer you stay, the more painful it is to leave. The same goes for email. Once you start to use Gmail as your default email, how likely are you to switch to another provider? Everything's there in Gmail already.

We might find the **annual model** in subscription services that bill annually. Sometimes just the annual reminder of being a customer causes the churn. Apart from the annual renewal decisions, this model describes churn that is flat the rest of the time. Churn in the annual model may also be higher than expected given that credit card details change over time. Some customers for business subscriptions are lost as they change jobs and don't take the subscription with them.

We often find the **cliffs model** in mobile app downloads and games. It is common to download a new app or game for a quick try only for users to find that it's not a fit for them. They then churn away. This behavior tends to make conversions to paid customers more expensive.

I also see something like this when a new service of any type gains a lot of awareness among readers of large tech publications. The readers are more likely than normal to try any new service. They're not really potential customers -- they just like to try new things. After they have tried it, then churn away.

# Why You Probably See a Less Deterministic Curve

In the early days, or when you have few customers, you won't be able to predict retention well. Your retention graphs will have sudden ups and downs. Some of that will be caused by randomness among small numbers of customers. Maybe one month you brought in customers that really needed your product. They might have high retention. You might find the opposite effect the next month.

The purpose of looking at retention data is predictability and improvement. Just also track the changes you and others make that could impact your retention.

A range of issues could cause future retention to be more chaotic. Let's look at a few.

**You haven't reached statistical significance**. With a small number of customers, the randomness of who happened to discover you and convert can sway the overall retention numbers.

**You have changed something substantial**. You've changed something big about your product suite. New pricing can produce changes to retention. A change in product offering can do the same.

**Different renewal patterns.** For subscription products, automatic billing reduces the decisions a customer needs to make in order to continue being a customer.

**You generate attention among a large group of non-customers**. Major press, whether formal publications or major blogs, will lead to this effect. When the article about your business is published and gains attention, thousands of new visitors become aware of your company and some sign up. This general effect for startups is sometimes called the TechCrunch bump (after the publication). Day one: a ton of new awareness and signups. Day two: a crash as the people who read about you (probably not your main customer target) churn away for the next new thing. Most of them weren't truly interested in what you built, they just wanted to try it out.

If you don't make a note of the TechCrunch bump or other similar events, later when you look at your retention, you might forget that you had a temporary surge in low quality customers. You'll think that something is wrong with your products, when you really just had more low quality conversions.

# Is Better Retention Actually Better?

What impacts retention? Many factors, including:
* Better understanding of who the target customer is, providing a solution for them, and pursuing customer acquisition there (higher retention).
* More coverage in general media, leading to both target and off-target customers being acquired (lower retention).
* Changes to price (higher or lower retention, depending on situation).
* Changes to customer communication (higher or lower retention, depending on situation). For example, keeping people engaged through regular communication. Or scaring people away by too frequent communication and reminding people that they should unsubscribe.
* Changes to product (higher or lower retention, depending on situation).
* Public opinion swayed for or against the business (higher or lower retention, depending on situation). For example, what happened during Uber's period of scandals where users deleted the app and went to Lyft or what happened to both increase and decrease support for Goya for political reasons.
* Entrance of competitors, changes in fashion, changes in demand, changes in economy... (higher or lower retention, depending on the situation).

And even among the factors where retention is improved, it is not always clear whether the improvement is better for the business.

It also stands to reason that the business, as it understands and focuses on its target customers, might also then have fewer target customers. They each might be more profitable for the business because of their longer retention, but the business overall might earn less because there are fewer customers total. Those off-target customers were worth something, after all. Some of those off-target customers later became target customers. Some of them also converted other people to become customers. So there can be cases where better retention actually makes things worse for the business. As with this entire book, you cannot take any one metric in isolation.

# Negative Churn

*If churn is just 1 - retention, can there be such a thing as negative churn?*

Churning away bad customers can be a good thing. This churn can improve average LTV (per channel or overall), improve referrals (good customers remain and have better things to say), and improve efficiency (good customers take less of your time). So some churn can be good.

But according to the way we defined retention above, churn is just 1 minus the retention rate. If retention is 95% in a period, then churn is 5%. So can there be such a thing as **negative churn**?

Negative churn occurs when even after losing customers in a period the customers who remain end up spending more (perhaps by upgrading or buying more) and the business ends up with more revenue per customer than previously. It's churn as measured on revenues or gross profit, not individual customers. Here's an example.

A business has 100 customers in a cohort in the current period, buying **on average** $10 worth of product. Revenue in that period is therefore $1,000. In the next period, 10% of the cohort's customers have churned away, leaving only 90 customers. However, those 90 customers spend on average $12 in the period. That means that revenue is now $1,080. That's higher revenue than earlier when the business had more customers in the cohort.

Customer retention may be 90%, but what is the churn on revenue?

*1 - ($1,080 / $1,000) = -8%*

Negative churn is a great thing. Good SaaS businesses, including Box, Dropbox, Google Drive, and others have it. You may also see negative churn referred to as positive net revenue retention.

# Matching LTV and CAC

## Time to Recover CAC
The typical calculation used to determine the months required to recover your CAC is:

*CAC / (Average revenue per customer per month - Cost to serve customer per month)*

With sample numbers from the below spreadsheet:

*Months to recover CAC = $50 to acquire the customer / ($10 - $3) = 7.1 months*

We need to wait until the 8th month after acquiring the customer until we have paid off just the CAC.

| Month | 0 | 1 | 2 | 3 | 4 | 5 | 6 | 7 | 8 | 9 | 10 | 11 | 12 |
|---|---|---|---|---|---|---|---|---|---|---|---|---|---|
| Revenue | | 10 | 10 | 10 | 10 | 10 | 10 | 10 | 10 | 10 | 10 | 10 | 10 |
| Costs | -50 | -3 | -3 | -3 | -3 | -3 | -3 | -3 | -3 | -3 | -3 | -3 | -3 |
| Gross Profit | | 7 | 7 | 7 | 7 | 7 | 7 | 7 | 7 | 7 | 7 | 7 | 7 |
| Cumulative | -50 | -43 | -36 | -29 | -22 | -15 | -8 | -1 | 6 | 13 | 20 | 27 | 34 |

However, this simple calculation is per retained customer. Overall, the calculation is guaranteed to be misleading until we add in retention.

If instead retention is 95% monthly, then our payback actually takes until the 9th month. In the below spreadsheet I compound the retention and costs at 95% each month to represent the steady loss of customers, their revenues, and costs.

We still recoup the $50 CAC, but instead of a constant $7/month we recoup less and less each month and much less by the end of the year.

| Month | 0 | 1 | 2 | 3 | 4 | 5 | 6 | 7 | 8 | 9 | 10 | 11 | 12 |
|---|---|---|---|---|---|---|---|---|---|---|---|---|---|
| Retention | | 100% | 95% | 95% | 95% | 95% | 95% | 95% | 95% | 95% | 95% | 95% | 95% |
| Revenue | | 10.00 | 9.50 | 9.03 | 8.57 | 8.15 | 7.74 | 7.35 | 6.98 | 6.63 | 6.30 | 5.99 | 5.69 |
| Costs | -50 | -3.00 | -2.85 | -2.71 | -2.57 | -2.44 | -2.32 | -2.21 | -2.10 | -1.99 | -1.89 | -1.80 | -1.71 |
| Gross Profit | | 7.00 | 6.65 | 6.32 | 6.00 | 5.70 | 5.42 | 5.15 | 4.89 | 4.64 | 4.41 | 4.19 | 3.98 |
| Cumulative | -50 | -43.00 | -36.35 | -30.03 | -24.03 | -18.33 | -12.91 | -7.77 | -2.88 | 1.77 | 6.18 | 10.37 | 14.35 |

# Using Discount Rates

*What are discount rates? Should you use discount rates?*

In our examples here, a discount rate is an assumption about the future value of payments. We take the value of getting paid $1 in the future to be less than getting paid today, for a couple reasons.

**The Time Value of Money**. Apart from uncommon situations where there is deflation instead of inflation, it's usually the case that $1 today is worth more than $1 tomorrow. We're also not counting the fact that some things become less expensive in the future (effects from Moore's Law or more efficient production). If we wait to buy things we also need to do without them in the present. So rather than inflation, the bigger loss can be when a business cannot use the revenue generated until it receives it later. Times of high inflation take their toll. Businesses that expect inflation to be consistently low can have their business models upended when inflation rises.

**Uncertainty Risk**. This is often the much larger part of a discount rate. Most new businesses fail. Projections aren't met. Loans go unpaid. Customers don't buy a new product that the business invested in producing. Customers go out of business. Uncertainty about the future typically makes up the majority of the discount rate.

This isn't a book about startup valuations. I admit that I usually avoid using discount rates. Related to uncertainty, I'm usually looking at potential companies and products that are quite risky but what the actual discount rate should be is subjective and based on many assumptions. Small differences in assumptions, carried years forward, will have big impacts on the way you look at an opportunity.

In general usage, discount rates may be around 10% for a low-risk public company, 15% - 25% for companies with small revenues (say in the tens of millions) demonstrating stability and predictability in their growth, higher for private companies without any sign of predictability, even higher for smaller, risky startups. I have heard of discount rates of 75% for extra-risky cannabis-related startups.

Discount rates introduce another level of complexity into your calculations. They do make sense, since you want to value a dollar received now more than one received later. But unless I want to test an LTV model with projections past a couple years, I often avoid using them to keep things simple.

Here is a sample to see how this would work. This sample shows an annual discount rate of 20%, spread over each month.

The formula to do that is 1 plus the discount rate over 12 months in a year to the power of the month number - 1:

*(1 + annual discount rate/12) ^ (month - 1)*

The impact I show is on the monthly gross profit, which is then modified as:

*gross profit in month / monthly discount rate*

Otherwise, the chart is the same as above. When you look at the totals, you see that it now takes until month 10 to recover CAC.

| Month | 0 | 1 | 2 | 3 | 4 | 5 | 6 | 7 | 8 | 9 | 10 | 11 | 12 |
|---|---|---|---|---|---|---|---|---|---|---|---|---|---|
| Retention | | 100% | 95% | 95% | 95% | 95% | 95% | 95% | 95% | 95% | 95% | 95% | 95% |
| Revenue | | 10.00 | 9.50 | 9.03 | 8.57 | 8.15 | 7.74 | 7.35 | 6.98 | 6.63 | 6.30 | 5.99 | 5.69 |
| Costs | -50 | -3.00 | -2.85 | -2.71 | -2.57 | -2.44 | -2.32 | -2.21 | -2.10 | -1.99 | -1.89 | -1.80 | -1.71 |
| Gross Profit | | 7.00 | 6.65 | 6.32 | 6.00 | 5.70 | 5.42 | 5.15 | 4.89 | 4.64 | 4.41 | 4.19 | 3.98 |
| Discount Rate | 20% | 1.00 | 1.02 | 1.03 | 1.05 | 1.07 | 1.09 | 1.10 | 1.12 | 1.14 | 1.16 | 1.18 | 1.20 |
| Discounted Gross Profit | | 7.00 | 6.54 | 6.11 | 5.71 | 5.34 | 4.99 | 4.66 | 4.35 | 4.07 | 3.80 | 3.55 | 3.32 |
| Cumulative | -50 | -43.00 | -36.46 | -30.35 | -24.64 | -19.30 | -14.31 | -9.65 | -5.30 | -1.23 | 2.57 | 6.13 | 9.44 |

# Projecting Inflation

*Should you factor inflation into your calculations?*

In our examples so far we didn't consider the impact of inflation on LTV or CAC. Let's add it in.

Here's a view showing what happens with inflation. The business previously expected no inflation (or inflation small enough not to matter) but now inflation is 12% per year.

In this situation, you might see the following impact. A business' costs increase as a result of inflation, but in this situation the business cannot also increase its prices yet.

This may be because the business committed to its prices in advance.

| Month | 0 | 1 | 2 | 3 | 4 | 5 | 6 | 7 | 8 | 9 | 10 | 11 | 12 |
|---|---|---|---|---|---|---|---|---|---|---|---|---|---|
| Retention | | 100% | 100% | 100% | 100% | 100% | 100% | 100% | 100% | 100% | 100% | 100% | 100% |
| Revenue | | 10.00 | 10.00 | 10.00 | 10.00 | 10.00 | 10.00 | 10.00 | 10.00 | 10.00 | 10.00 | 10.00 | 10.00 |
| Annual Inflation Rate | 12% | 1.00 | 1.01 | 1.02 | 1.03 | 1.04 | 1.05 | 1.06 | 1.07 | 1.08 | 1.09 | 1.10 | 1.12 |
| Costs (assumes no inflation) | -50 | -3.00 | -3.00 | -3.00 | -3.00 | -3.00 | -3.00 | -3.00 | -3.00 | -3.00 | -3.00 | -3.00 | -3.00 |
| Costs (actuals with inflation) | -50 | -3.00 | -3.03 | -3.06 | -3.09 | -3.12 | -3.15 | -3.18 | -3.22 | -3.25 | -3.28 | -3.31 | -3.35 |
| Gross Profit (assumed no inflation) | | 7.00 | 7.00 | 7.00 | 7.00 | 7.00 | 7.00 | 7.00 | 7.00 | 7.00 | 7.00 | 7.00 | 7.00 |
| Gross Profit with Inflation | | 7.00 | 6.93 | 6.86 | 6.79 | 6.73 | 6.66 | 6.59 | 6.53 | 6.46 | 6.40 | 6.34 | 6.27 |
| GP Totals without Inflation | -50 | -43.00 | -36.00 | -29.00 | -22.00 | -15.00 | -8.00 | -1.00 | 6.00 | 13.00 | 20.00 | 27.00 | 34.00 |
| GP Totals with Inflation | -50 | -43.00 | -36.07 | -29.21 | -22.41 | -15.69 | -9.03 | -2.43 | 4.10 | 10.56 | 16.96 | 23.30 | 29.57 |

Note how things change if costs increase while the business can't keep increasing its prices similarly. In this example, I'm using 12% annual inflation, which delivers a small amount of inflation month over month. At year end, expected (no inflation) vs actual (with inflation) produces different gross profits.

You could also see specific costs temporarily increase beyond that of inflation (for example, as shipping became much more expensive during COVID or as certain microchips became in short supply). Models that worked in previous years now fall apart.

# What We Can Try to Control About CAC and LTV

In the above sections, these are the levers that we can try to push to improve CAC and LTV.

## CAC

- Lower the cost to bring someone "in the door" if you can still gain "good" customers.
- Increase the conversion rate of potential customers by avoiding the ones that aren't a fit or better explaining your value to the ones who are a fit.
- Track and understand the differences in CAC across different channels.
- Track changes across time.
- Understand the CAC payback period for different segments and at difference prices.
- Understand the connection between customers acquired through different channels and their eventual LTV.

## LTV

- Improve pricing. Improvement could mean increasing or decreasing prices, depending on situation and goals.
- Improve margins (costs).
- Improve retention.
- Understand how LTV is like a river. When are payments received and how long it takes to pay back CAC.

## Overall

- Understand the value of segmenting vs averaging customers.
- Appreciate outliers as opportunities to gain insight.
- Graph your data to help you notice other changes.

# Business Type Case Studies

*"There are four kinds of business: Tourism. Food service. Railroads, and sales. And hospitals slash manufacturing. And air travel...."* -- Michael Scott, in The Office

There are many types of business.

But what's a business model? I like the definition from Ash Maurya, the creator of the Lean Canvas, who states that a business model describes the value a company produces for its customers, how it captures value, and the costs of providing value. It's a good definition in that it's complete and simple to explain part by part. The business model is sustainable if each of those parts is larger than the next. That is, if the value produced is greater than the value captured and the value captured is greater than the cost to provide the value.

How many different business models can you think of?

Depending on how much time you took you may have come up with five, 10, 20 or more. This list might include advertising, data, pay-what-you-wish, retail, subscription, consulting, cost-plus, non-profit, donations, razors-and-blades, licensing, retail, and more.

One way to look at business models is to group them into categories. Ash Maurya also says that there are really only three categories of business model: **direct** (the business sells directly to its customers), **indirect** (the business provides a service for users and then sells access to those users), and **marketplace** (matching buyers and sellers).

For thinking through the way the businesses themselves behave, Maurya's three types work. But in this book we're going to look at case studies of many different businesses that fall into one or more of those types. And even if the business model types have fundamental similarities, applied to different businesses, there may be differences in CAC or LTV. Going into these case studies also shows just how many variations there are on ways businesses operate (and the following is just a short list).

I also chose my list to include both some popular and unusual businesses. I hope that the comparison helps you think through other business types that you encounter.

# Mattresses: Bricks-and-Mortar and Online

One common business is the mattress store. Whether bricks-and-mortar storefronts or online direct-to-consumer (D2C), there are a lot of these businesses. For a purchase that is rarely made, why should mattress stores be so common?

The answer lies in the unit economics of a mattress. While it is an infrequent purchase, a mattress generates hundreds of dollars of gross profit -- sometimes even more than an automobile dealer earns from a sale price 20 to 30 times higher. At the same time, traditional mattress stores don't require much more than a basic storefront, some inventory, and a salesperson. The number of sales needed to keep a small store open is quite low.

Additionally, we've recently seen the growth in online D2C mattress brands such as Casper, Tuft & Needle, Leesa, Purple Mattress, and GhostBed. No stores, so they ship the mattress directly to your home.

Let's look at mattresses in general and then each business type in turn.

Mattress gross margins can be in the 50% - 60% range, which as a percentage isn't uncommon in retail. What's uncommon is the price point. Mattresses often sell at around $1,000. That means that if a mattress store is taking $600 gross on the sale of a single mattress, they don't need to sell all that many to stay in business. One estimate (from a Freakonomics interview) of the sales needed came to just "a dozen to 20 mattresses a month to essentially cover their costs." Less than one sale a day to keep the store open.

Being infrequent purchases, mattress companies traditionally didn't have much of a customer relationship. But could that change when purchases move online?

A D2C mattress company that now knows who bought, when they bought, where they live, and more can use this information. Past brick-and-mortar mattress companies could not collect this data, except possibly in the aggregate (look at market research on how people buy and who buys). But since the new D2C mattress companies have these additional data points and a way to contact their customers, they can follow up with them to upsell other items based on individual age or family composition. They can use their customers as a channel to reach new customers (incentivizing sharing a referral or a coupon). They can extend into other sleep and home related products. It doesn't matter if they move.

The potential value of this business type is different from that of a bricks-and-mortar mattress brand. For example, Target discussed buying online mattress company Casper for $1B in 2017. Online mattress companies have sold billions of dollars of mattresses in a short time.

But Casper, just to pick on one of the D2C mattress companies that went public, does not look like a good business. Its 2019 revenue was $440 million and gross margin was 49% (which can be good), but its Sales and Marketing Expense ($155 million) and General and Administrative Expenses ($150 million) are significant and there are still other costs too. To give you a rough example of how bad it is, consider this. For every $1,000 mattress that Casper sells, it costs the company $1,200 overall. That's a dramatic difference to the bricks-and-mortar retailers. Shouldn't Casper be more efficient than the traditional businesses?

There's a lot going on in their annual report, but the basic reasons are these:
1. It's not trivial to manage the shipments, returns, and customer problems with large, heavy items like mattresses.
2. Without bricks-and-mortar stores and many online competitors, Casper needs to spend on online advertising. Acquiring a customer for an expensive and infrequent purchase where there are also many other competitors quickly becomes expensive.
3. With a lot of money raised ($340 million as a private company, not including their IPO) Casper has the budget to spend on customer acquisition. It doesn't really need to be efficient right now. Not the case for brick-and-mortar mattress stores, which would close if they couldn't cover costs.

It's still early in the days of D2C mattress companies. But Casper is just one example of too much funding and a competitive environment leading a company to prioritize growth over efficiency. At least for a while.

Note that while Casper's CAC (using Sales and Marketing Expense as the estimate) is currently 72% of its LTV ($155 million vs $215 million in gross profit). Its other costs of running the business account for the overall loss. Things could improve over the years if Casper retains its customers for future purchases.

Note that in a COVID-19 environment, brick-and-mortar mattress stores should be at a disadvantage to their online competitors. But that might mean that both types of mattress store are in for difficulties.

61

# Subscription and Freemium: Data Storage, Movies, and More

Subscription business models are built on high-retention. Customers sometimes receive more value the longer they use the product. Variations include content (paid newsletters, music, and video) and services (file storage, design software, and operating system software).

Some subscription businesses try to improve their customer retention by making their services more useful the longer you use them, or even addictive. In the first case, we call that customer lock-in. In other words, customers find it difficult to switch away from the subscription service because their data is stored there and hard to move, they know how to use the service and don't know how to use others, or other reasons. Addiction refers to the way that many services design themselves for repeat usage, including adding notifications, variable rewards, and more.

Subscription businesses also have the potential for negative churn, as we described above in the Retention section of this book. That's where the retained customers spend more and more than make up for the lost customers who churn away.

Some subscription businesses are also known for forcing or encouraging their customers into high retention. They require customers to call by phone in order to cancel, as for example the NY Times and others. Others work through a script of discounts when customers don't renew an annual subscription, as for example The Information and others.

Free users receive restricted content and services while paid customers receive full content and services.    Small numbers of users upgrade to paid. Retention can be high for both free and paid users. Free trial periods help free users understand the benefits and possibly upgrade. Product lock-in (significant personal data and contacts captured) means that it is hard to switch to other services.

What qualities are important for a successful freemium service?
1. Wide appeal (enough people in the funnel to upgrade to paid).
2. Managing the costs of the free accounts.
3. Generating revenue even from free accounts, for example through advertising.
4. Retaining enough of the free and paid accounts.

Many freemium services are also subscription-based, given that they offer people limited features for free. But others also function as one-off purchases.

## Free Publicity

Some businesses manage customer awareness well. Some are the long running, large brands that already have deep relationships with the press and can push marketing campaigns more efficiently than newer or small companies.

Some businesses actually require free publicity for their businesses to work as well as they do. Let's look at a few examples of companies doing it well and not so well.

## MoviePass

MoviePass was a movie theater subscription service that started operations in 2011. Starting in 2018 they offered something too good to be true: $9.95 per month to be able to watch a movie in a theater each day of the month. And apparently, apart from that, there was no hidden revenue stream. By that I mean that other than the monthly subscription fees, MoviePass did not also generate revenue in another way, for example by claiming back a percentage of movie theater concession sales. The revenue model did however go through several revisions over 2018.

First, MoviePass offered $9.95/month for unlimited movies at participating theaters.

It took two days for MoviePass to add 150,000 subscribers to this plan. The figure is notable because this is the number of subscribers at which MoviePass management would receive a $2 million bonus. (They thought it would take a year to reach that subscriber number. The bonus paid out as long as they hit the number in 18 months.)

In terms of driving down CAC, they did the right thing. The newsworthiness of one movie a day for $9.95/month meant that MoviePass gained lots of attention. Beyond moving CAC to zero, MoviePass also served a large market (from regular to occasional moviegoers).

The question then was, what was LTV? And would anything about historical movie theater consumption change?

At the time, the US average price of a movie ticket was $8.73 (higher in many urban areas) and amazingly, MoviePass had to pay full price back to the theaters. So if people only went to one movie per month, MoviePass would have a gross profit of $1.22 each month ($9.95 - $8.73). Before

MoviePass, people tended to only go to four to five movies per year. The assumption was that even if frequency doubled to 10 movies per year, MoviePass would be ahead. But what if their calculations were off? The company earlier had priced the same product at $35/month.

According to an industry report, average customers of AMC movie theaters spent $5.29 per month on concessions. A question was how that spending would change as subscription customers saw more movies per month. Some reports showed that movie ticket subscriptions increase per visit spending. If you show up at the theater having already bought the ticket online, you feel less like you've spent money and then make up for it by buying more concessions.

Whereas the old model was one ticket for one movie, a flat fee model that estimated potential behavior is riskier. It does have the potential to increase revenues, but it also has the risk of serving free-loaders. That is, the people who buy MoviePass are those who already go to many movies each month. That's why using average movie-going behavior is misleading for a business of this type.

The other change was that after MoviePass proved that there was demand, large movie theater chains rolled out their own subscription plans.

MoviePass expected to be able to sell customer data as a second revenue stream, but that didn't happen, showing that there are more companies talking about selling data than there are companies actually selling data.

MoviePass management did the right thing -- for their bonuses. But services like MoviePass can also attract the most frequent moviegoers (who save money without changing behavior) and move the next most frequent moviegoers up in their viewership. Companies in this situation end up attracting their least profitable customers.

MoviePass' parent company spent $100 million supporting their subscription service. Monthly losses kept growing. They then limited new members to four movies per month. But it was too late. Service ended in September 2019.

MoviePass' parent eventually delisted from Nasdaq.

**Data storage services**
Unlike the MoviePass example, data storage services (like file storage or hosted email) historically used a "skate to where the puck will be" strategy.

Sometimes there is predictable technological change that you can use to your advantage in industries where the current unit economics do not support building a business. Let's consider a long-running trend -- the reduction in the cost of data storage -- over the last 20 years.

Data storage is pretty boring, right? But data storage and its predictable fall in costs is also what enabled many companies to emerge before their unit economics made sense. Companies and products like Dropbox, Box, Evernote, and Gmail all provide their users with freemium data storage. They offer a free plan of limited storage along with paid plans for higher levels of storage.

In the case of Google's Gmail, upon beta launch in 2004, users gained an at-the-time unheard of 1 Gb in storage, for free. For the first year or so, Gmail throttled the number of signups by requiring new users to be invited by an existing user. At first 5 invitations were available per user, then 100, and then Gmail removed the throttle altogether. That allowed Gmail to ensure that the product worked with more people and to actually see how the product was used. A largely word of mouth CAC of $0.

But from a unit economics perspective, data storage companies started to offer their services before they seemed to make sense. Those free or even freemium plans didn't cover costs. But that actually did make sense over time. The reason was that the cost of data storage was declining at a predictable rate. By starting early, these companies already had users when the economics of data storage became profitable.

**Freemium data storage services**
*LTV free users = (revenue from ad CPM - cost to provide storage) X periods as user*

Some services do not display advertising and accept the free users as a necessary cost to finding the paid users.

*LTV paid users = (monthly fee - cost to provide storage) X months as user*

Remember that the cost of storage fell dramatically after these services launched. In the beginning they may have had a negative LTV, but a combination of predictable cost reduction plus investment got them through the negative years.

Some paid services still include advertising, so the formula may be modified accordingly. Those changes in the data storage industry looked like this chart.

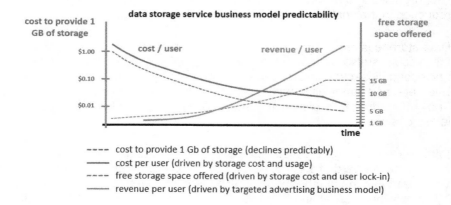

---- cost to provide 1 Gb of storage (declines predictably)
—— cost per user (driven by storage cost and usage)
---- free storage space offered (driven by storage cost and user lock-in)
—— revenue per user (driven by targeted advertising business model)

# Mobility: Taxi Medallions, Rideshare, Scooters, and Bikes

### Taxi Medallions

Historically, taxi medallions were good investments. A municipality would issue a set number of medallions and limit supply for what was often growing demand for transport. For example, New York City issued 15,000 taxi medallions in 1937. After some went unrenewed during the Great Depression, 13,000 remained. There are still around 13,000 taxi medallions in NYC today.

NYC taxi medallions ranged in price from $200K to $1M from the 1990s to 2015. Why did people buy them? A medallion gives the owner the right to drive or lease a taxi and generate an average income stream (after expenses) of around $50K per year. That $50K per year was pretty stable in the past since there were no new forms of transportation being developed. Apart from taxis, people in NYC could take the subway, buses, walk, and of course, drive their own cars – all forms of transportation that had been pretty stable (no major additions) for a long time.

That stability meant that the price of a taxi medallion was roughly equal to the $50K it could generate divided by the interest rate. In other words, that was the amount of money someone would have to deposit in order to gain $50K in interest. This meant that the price tended to go up when interest rates were low.

Taxi medallions were a good investment for a long time. It was an asset that generally held up or appreciated in value. And even if the asset did fall in value, owners could hold on to them, rent and sell their medallions later.

A medallion owner could think of the medallion as buying the right to acquire customers at a low CAC (the cost of driving in a crowded city with many potential fares). The market was controlled by a regulator that did not issue new medallions or allow other taxi companies to enter. So it made sense to buy a medallion.

There were only a couple things that could damage the value of a medallion:

- Timing mismatch. Substantial gas and other price increases that are not met by increased flag-fall and per mile and per-minute increases (all set by the regulator). There were times that were better or worse, but the regulator tended to adjust the taxi fare price increases somewhat in line with cost increases.

- A change in taxi demand. Predictable change was seasonal, time of day, and day of week. Less predictable was economic (fewer fares when riders have less money). Big public works projects, like subway line extensions were slow moving and didn't majorly impact ridership.
- Changing the protection of high demand routes. Subway travel to NYC airports and the Javits Center was not easy. That kept taxis central to those routes.

It took a few years for the impact to be felt and for medallion prices to plummet, but the stable system above changed when rideshare companies like Uber and Lyft showed up.

Uber and Lyft are businesses that depend on market share. That is, these businesses can work well when there is a limited number of providers. It makes less sense for each city to have its own rideshare company (and app) even though that is essentially what cities have when it comes to taxi companies. For rideshare businesses to work, they require some minimum level of market penetration. That's why we saw these companies expand to many geographies early.

**Car Rideshare vs Scooters**
Unlike the taxi examples above, a rideshare company like Uber or Lyft thinks more in terms of CAC and LTV and without regulation, can add as many drivers as they want.

Rideshare businesses requiring drivers with their own cars operate differently from scooter and bike alternatives. Car and driver based rideshare pushes many of the costs to the drivers. Drivers must pay for a vehicle, fuel, insurance, maintenance, and cleaning and of course the time and expense of driving their vehicle to pick up passengers.

With scooter and bike rideshare, the company pays for the vehicles, energy costs, maintenance, and location redeployment. Car rideshare has costs of attracting and retaining drivers where scooter and bike companies do not. The problem of new driver onboarding (and getting drivers faster than competitors) was significant enough that in the beginning, car rideshare companies sometimes paid bonuses (in the hundreds or thousands of dollars) to drivers after completing training and their first rides.

But after expenses, driver take-home pay tends to be about $10/hour, or basically minimum wage. Much worse than driving a taxi, though it also requires much less commitment.

It took a few years, but rideshare companies eventually became cheaper than a taxi, at least with their common cheaper options like Uber Pool. This does not necessarily mean that rideshare companies also became sustainable businesses.

For one thing, lower price points and higher levels of overhead show up in a few ways on Uber's annual report. Looking at Uber's most recent annual report, roughly 47% of "cost of revenue" items related to paying drivers, insurance, payment processing, regulations, and more. The next highest cost is for sales and marketing at 30%, R&D (another cost absent from taxi companies) is 15%, and more combine so that Uber loses money on a per rider basis. For Lyft, it's roughly 60% for cost of revenue, 22% for sales and marketing, and 41% for R&D. Lyft also loses money per ride on average. In other markets, the situation is similar too. Didi Chuxing, a China-based rideshare company, is also not profitable per ride.

This situation was almost unavoidable. The companies' management and investors organized around growth now and sustainability later. To go after the top one or two spot -- necessary in a winner take all market -- rideshare companies needed to grow whether the growth was sustainable or not.

But there are some other interesting and more optimistic components to these businesses.

First, rideshare passengers show negative churn (the customers retained spend more and make up for the ones who have churned). This may have changed in a time of COVID-19, but the negative churn looked promising pre-pandemic.

In a 2016 study, economists analyzed Uber data and drew their demand curve. It's relatively inelastic, meaning surge pricing does dissuade some riders, but the higher fees more than make up for dropped demand.

**Scooter Rentals**
Scooter rental is different from car-based rideshare in a few ways. First, the company itself must buy and manage the scooters. Car rideshare typically pushes the vehicle cost and fuel to drivers. Since there are no drivers to pay, the scooter companies must instead pay for battery charging themselves (whether they pay others to do it or manage it internally). So scooter companies have higher up front capital expenditures (the scooter purchases) while still having high operating costs.

They might still make sense as a business though.

How does the business model of a dockless scooter rental company like Bird or Lime work?

Dockless scooter rental businesses have been hot over the past few years, raising hundreds of millions of dollars. As with car-based rideshare, let's look at what needs to happen for investment in a single Bird scooter to break even.

The scooters, outfitted with GPS, assembled, with Bird branding, and shipping originally cost Bird $551 each. Since these scooters are left outside all day they have a much shorter lifespan than normal. They get damaged from the multiple rides, people intentionally damage them, they are out in the sun and rain, and more.

So how many days does a scooter need to remain functional in order to pay back its cost and breakeven?

To calculate time to breakeven on a scooter, we have the following:

*Cost of scooter / ((trips per day X revenue per trip) - (cost to charge per day + maintenance cost per day + regulatory fees))*

Note that scooter companies weren't necessarily able to negotiate manufacturer discounts given how much money poured into this industry and sudden increased demand. Based on estimates for average revenue per trip and an estimated 3 to 5 trips before the scooter needs a charge, we have the following:

*$551 scooter costs / ((5 trips/day X $3.50/trip) - ($5 charging cost/day + $0.50 maintenance + $0.25 regulatory fees)) = 47 days*

(If the above calculation is run with only 3 rides per charge, the number of days until break event is 116.)

Run the optimistic calculation above on the lower scooter cost and we have:

*$360 scooter costs / ((5 trips/day X $3.50/trip) - ($5 charging cost/day + $0.50 maintenance + $0.25 regulatory fees)) = 31 days*

So there are paths for a scooter company to reach break even. Depending on whether the scooters do last that long, which may not be the case at least in some markets.

If scooter companies could either reduce the purchase price, improve the battery so that it doesn't need as many charges, or improve the durability of the scooters so that they last longer, they would also be better businesses. Increasing the price to ride could impact demand, but is also a way to improve their situation.

For these reasons, investors in scooter companies deemed them to be good investments. Time will tell.

**Dockless Bike Rentals**
Seems like we've already covered much of the transportation sharing economy, but I'm keeping bikes as a separate section. The reason is over the past few years we saw several very highly funded companies like Mobike, Ofo, and Lime emerge in dockless bikeshare. (As with scooters, dockless bikes can be parked and picked up anywhere -- users find and pay for the bikes via an app). Dockless bike rollouts went from near zero to millions of units in a span of one year -- 2017.

The main differences between dockless bikes and scooters were in the way the devices work. Bikes were cheaper, more producers could manufacture them, did not require battery recharging, and had more of an argument around greening the city in which they operated. Though, like scooters, the bikes also did clutter streets and produce waste.

That's why it's not surprising that some dockless bike companies also raised tremendous amounts of capital, spread millions of bikes around cities, and eventually shut down. This too was a winner take all market. But the business model was a tougher one. Too much expenditure on capital and revenue too small per bike to make up for it. In some estimates, the bikes never break even.

# Consumer Packaged Goods (CPG)

Consumer packaged goods (CPG) are items that consumers regularly use and which also require routine replacement, such as food, beverages, clothes, cosmetics, and other household products.

CPG companies produce a product and often sell it either direct to consumer (D2C) or via retail stores. CPG is very diverse in product types and there are multiple industries that themselves support the CPG industry. CPG is much bigger than tech and yet many people don't know how it works.

Very basically, there are a few stages to roll out a CPG product. Often this starts with an R&D phase which, depending on product, includes everything from flavor formulation, branding, and customer tests. Traditionally, CPG companies were slow and thoughtful about new products to release. However, they have increasingly sped up the time to market for test products and changed their distribution tactics. One multinational CPG company I advised was able to reduce their concept to shelf timeline from 18 months to around three months for test products.

Also, over the last few years we've seen more small, independent CPG companies emerge, either serving a niche and remaining independent, or becoming an acquisition target for a larger brand. For example, many artisanal beer brands have been acquired by the handful of large alcohol companies, like AmBev and 3G, even if they still appear as different brands.

Many people outside the industry don't know that CPG product margins can be substantial. As a result, it can be common for some brands to spend more on marketing than on the products' cost of goods sold (COGS).

People out of the industry often don't know how CPG companies reach their customers. Since CPG products tend to be on the less expensive side (compared to larger less frequent purchases, like housing, automotive, electronics, etc) large companies are built around having many customers who buy many times. For a CPG company, investing in the brand pays off in retention.

Historically, large CPG companies reached customers via presence in thousands of retail stores, typically not their own. Ecommerce also became an important customer channel, though it is still small compared to brick-and-mortar retail. Then, as CPG companies started to look for ways to give up less value, they started to sell direct to consumer (D2C).

For some new companies, like Dollar Shave Club, running a successful D2C company required managing free publicity, customer referrals, developing subscription plans to keep retention high, and a lot of paid advertising. Over time, retaining the best customers might also lead to negative churn. Doing this with a niche product is easier than with a mainstream one, which is why some new brands also stall out at a certain size.

A D2C sales channel often means that the CPG company ships products directly to the customer's home and has a relationship with their customers (knowing their demographics, likes and dislikes, past orders, email, phone number, and home address). The CPG company selling D2C must also manage customer relationships, meaning that customer service, returns, and identifying new ways to upsell are important risks and opportunities for them.

In retail, some small and mid-sized companies go through wholesalers and distributors just to get shelf space. The wholesalers manage the retailer relationship and distributors manage the logistical challenge to keep the product stocked. They also take a cut of sales and other fees.

The following is a very rough representative breakdown as the product moves from producer to retailer to customer. Skew the numbers more when more intermediaries are added.

- If the *COGS* (the cost of goods sold paid by the CPG company) is around $2.50, then the
- *Wholesale Price* (the price paid to the CPG company by the retailer) will be around $5, and the
- *Retail Price* (paid by the customer) will be $10.

(Those of you with CPG experience know that I have left out a lot. To keep the models simple, I'm not including other costs in retail CPG like stocking fees paid for the retailer to add a product to their inventory, free samples to convince the retailers to accept their products, and different pricing based on product placement within the store. These costs can be substantial, depending on the brand, competition, and how well the products have already proven to sell. But in the end I left them out since they vary so much depending on the situation.)

The other factor to remember is when and how producers get paid. Again typically, retailers pay the CPG companies after customers buy the product. If items are unsold, retailers may return them to the CPG company (sometimes with a cost). They also might sometimes have to dispose of items that are damaged or expired.

That means that the CPG companies, especially new ones, need to be aware of the timing of payments for selling via retailers. They may sell more product via retailers, but if the CPG company cannot wait the several months it may take to get paid, they will find it difficult to grow. Large, established retailers can deal with the timing issue, may negotiate better terms, or may have better margins. Smaller CPG companies may fail or find it hard to grow even if people want their products because they cannot deal with the delay in payment.

## CPG Product Sold in Retail Store

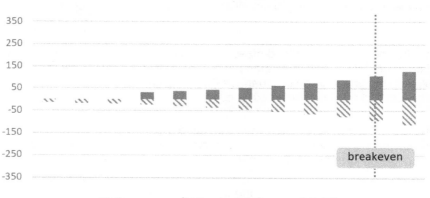

■ Revenue (Wholesale)  ⧤ COGS

The retail sales example has the CPG company paid after a delay of three months.

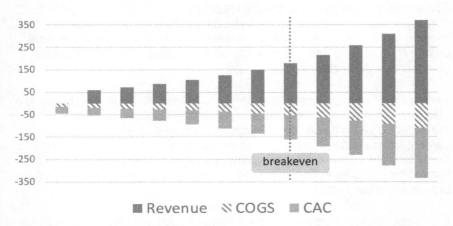

CPG Product Direct to Consumer

■ Revenue ⬚ COGS ■ CAC

The D2C example has the CPG company paid after one month. In this scenario, the CPG company also incurs a CAC, which it does not have in the retail example. This is not a perfect replica of reality since many companies selling via retailers do incur marketing costs, just not costs that are directly associated with each customer acquired. In my example, I'm keeping the gross margins plus CAC the same in each case.

If you can manage the gross margin and timing issues, you might have a good business.

# Ecommerce: Centralizing Supply and Demand

Ecommerce is still just 15% of total retail sales, though with predictions that sales will increasingly move online in a COVID-19 environment. The general model for ecommerce companies is to aggregate products (their own or from others) and to then capture a percentage fee of the goods sold through the platform.

Sellers on ecommerce sites give up some of their revenue, potentially in a combination of per product fees and percentages of the sale price. Why do the sellers give up those fees? Because it's a cost of going where the customers are, similar to bricks-and-mortar retail. Producers exchange those fees for increased sales volume, possibly less expense and time to market their goods, and in some cases, less time to set themselves up as producers in the first place.

Large ecommerce companies like Amazon added other services such as warehousing and order fulfillment in exchange for additional fees. For some smaller producers, paying these higher rates makes sense too.

Historically, ecommerce businesses had retention problems. Customers didn't visit an ecommerce site except when they needed to buy something. Potential customers might check multiple sites.

Amazon improved its customer retention by expanding offerings to include just about anything. Amazon and others also added subscriptions for physical products (automatically reorder a product you have purchased in the past) which customers agreed to for a price discount (and the simplicity) as well as subscriptions for digital services, like video streaming, that in general are priced as monthly all-you-can-watch. Another service, AWS hosting, is usage-based, but where customers typically infrequently change their hosting provider.

Through this process, the Amazon homepage became the search box for products. Amazon also created Amazon Prime as a $119/year fee that brings other consumption benefits (free and faster shipping, reduced purchase prices, free content etc). Amazon Prime Student at $59/year is a way to gain access to customers before they have as much disposable income, build a habit with them, and then charge them more as they graduate at predictable rates.

These changes improved both retention (customers stay and buy more often) and also potentially gross margin (customers shop around for better deals less often).

Like the traditional retailers, ecommerce companies benefit from paying out to their producers only after the products have been sold. In some extreme cases, the ecommerce company can reduce its prices to the cost of the products and still make money. That's the magic of the float and payment terms.

Making money from the float requires the ecommerce company to transact large sums in the forms of payments in (and out), to have access to those deposits for some amount of time (they can sit in an Amazon bank account), and in the most basic case, those deposits can generate interest.

Even without the float, large ecommerce companies benefit from payment terms. Amazon and Walmart, for example, have large negative accounts payable, meaning that they collect payments from customers before they need to pay out to suppliers and sellers. This is a recipe for growth.

It is hard to displace a marketplace once it is built. If anything, ecommerce marketplaces become stronger over time. They are able to add new product lines and even develop their own products in-house that they can later sell on their platform, competing with their own sellers. For sellers, going to a marketplace as the main source of customers might be a faster way to grow (higher volumes, lower CAC) but also presents a lot of risk in that the environment can suddenly change.

# Returns: A Byproduct

Sometimes a customer buys a product, but then decides that they do not want it. This could be because the product doesn't work, doesn't fit (especially related to clothing, shoes, and eyewear), or is not what they expected.

Returns are a byproduct of a few other changes. Over a couple centuries ago, almost all products were produced artisanally. Clothing and many other products were custom made (even if the textiles and other materials were mass produced). Pick out the fabric, discuss the style, and return over a series of visits for tailoring (or make them at home). Not knowing that something didn't fit wasn't a problem.

Mass manufacturing of consumable goods with international supply chains changed that. Improved gross margins meant that it became cheaper to overproduce goods that were good enough for most potential buyers (a set number of sizes, colors, styles). In the present day, the ease of shopping and paying for something online prioritizes the sale, rather than the "right" sale. The result was that many items are returned. And even so, companies can thrive in that situation.

Rough estimates are that buyers return 30% of products bought online (clothing accounts for a large part of that), as compared to 9% of products returned in brick-and-mortar retailers.

That retailers, both online and brick-and-mortar, even allow an option for easy returns depends on their good margins and the desire to keep customer retention high. That creates the need to do something with the returned items.

Given that returns are sometimes worn or broken, the retailer might not be able to resell them. The question then becomes how to generate value from items that otherwise have no worth.

So an outcome of returns is that there is a market for people to buy pallets of returned products and then to sort and sell them.

Why would a retailer not sell these items themselves? Some jobs are better done by others. A major retailer like Amazon can find it to be better business to sell a pallet of mixed items to individuals who will take the time to sort and resell them, than it would be to store the items for longer in their warehouse.

The business of selling returned items also relies on buyers thinking that they can do better than the purchase price. This is not always the case.

There is a COVID-19 impact on the number of returns, given that more shopping moved online during the pandemic. If the pandemic impacts buyers economically, returns may be higher as well.

# Organized Crime: Illegal Drug Trade

Unit economics of the illegal drug trade relies on a few things.

- Very cheap production of raw materials, often in remote areas that are difficult to control (remote areas of Colombia, Afghanistan, Myanmar, for example).
- A very high (relative to the costs) retail price for the drugs.
- Levels of addiction (retention) that keep people buying in spite of prices or illegality.
- A path to customers that often involves many intermediaries. This is often because the drugs themselves are bulky and noticeable in quantities.

In some cases, drugs sell at retail for many times the cost of materials. A very rough calculation for cocaine looks like this:

- Approximately $1 - $1.50/kilo for coca leaves, which are not that potent themselves and which need to be processed.
- Approximately $550 - 750/kilo for coca leaves concentrated and processed into cocaine base, which is then inexpensively processed into usable cocaine.
- $2000/kilo for cocaine in remote areas in Colombia close to production.
- $7,000/kilo for cocaine at Colombian ports before export.
- Approximately $70,000/kilo retail for cocaine in the US (varying based on location).

Taking just the second step in the above list as the first point usable cocaine is produced, that's a 100 fold increase from materials cost to retail price. The dramatic difference goes to a wide series of middlemen who transport, package, and sell the product to customers, often risking their lives in the process.

Some of this has changed in recent years as synthetic drugs like fentanyl can be produced at tiny costs per dose, can produce margins at low price points, and can be shipped directly to consumers. D2C shipments for drugs like fentanyl change the game and are difficult to police. Unfortunately, their unit economics make their spread inevitable.

Looking at the drug trade through the lens of this book and you see good LTV (high gross margins), low CAC, and high customer retention. Without that, who would put up with the difficulty and risk?

# Parasites: Ransomware and Spam

Ransomware groups operate a kind of business. It's a business based on targeting companies, accessing their private data, encrypting it to preserve it in an unusable state, and then demanding payment for the encryption keys.

Ransomware attacks can come and go without many people knowing -- unless they target consumer-facing companies and the story more easily becomes public. Garmin, a maker of GPS-related navigation, tracking, and fitness apps, was a well-known ransomware target in mid-2020. As a result, some Garmin services were down for about a week after the company apparently declined to pay the $10 million ransom. The group believed to be behind the Garmin attack was notably called Evil Corp and is based in Russia.

Bringing down much of a multibillion dollar business' operations for a week is certainly very expensive. So why not just pay the $10 million to make the problem go away? That would protect Garmin's customers, stock price, and reputation.

Garmin and other US-based targets of ransomware legally can't just pay a sanctioned company. The US Treasury had already sanctioned Evil Corp which created penalties for transacting with them (that is, paying the ransomware bribe).

According to the US Treasury Department:

*"[A]ll property and interests in property of these persons subject to U.S. jurisdiction are blocked, and U.S. persons are generally prohibited from engaging in transactions with them…. Foreign persons may be subject to secondary sanctions for knowingly facilitating a significant transaction or transactions with these designated persons."*

The ransomware business model (pay for the keys to restore your encrypted data) has a good CAC to LTV tradeoff but seems to keep hacker ambition low. Imagine the value unlocked if instead they could affect election results, impact stock prices, or more.

Since ransomware is often spread by phone and email phishing attacks that trick employees into revealing account information, the cost to get someone "in the door" (to make an analogy to the CAC equation) is small. The conversion rate is also small, given that company security infrastructure and policies often keep potential ransomware attackers away.

Later reports claim that Garmin actually did pay the fee, believing that it was initiated by a different hacker group.

### Spam
We usually think of spam as malevolent -- a scam that parts fools with their money. But actually, spamming just means contacting (often emailing) many non-subscribed people with commercial offerings. Many successful startups started with small-scale spam to grow awareness.

Why do they do it? Well, if you have access to an email list, or if you can build one, for example by scraping emails posted online, or even by taking all of your contacts (and your friends contacts), you have a list of people to market to without any cost. That's alluring to many early-stage businesses that have no budget.

That type of spam is also based on the desire to lower CAC for what may otherwise be a good product. It's a smaller, friendlier, less predatory version of what we unusually think of as spam.

A business can't keep that up forever, though. If enough recipients mark the messages as spam, email providers will proactively place messages from the company's domain in the spam folder. Then the company will have difficulty reaching anyone.

There is also malevolent spam. That is, spam sent with the intention to deceive and scam money from strangers.

Note that for bad spam especially, many of the messages include typos. The belief is that spammers intentionally use typos in their messages to improve their conversion rates. That is, make the message seem unprofessional in order not to have to deal with the more savvy recipient who is just going to waste the spammers' time. If someone doesn't notice the typos, then they could convert at a higher rate.

Spam is an unusual type of business in that it is so lopsided between value created and cost incurred. The value created (well, money stolen) was estimated by Justin M. Rao of Microsoft Research and David H. Reiley of Google in a 2012 paper titled "The Economics of Spam."

From the research, just in the US, the value created for spammers was estimated at around $200 million. The cost incurred by non-spammers (wasted time, extra software and equipment) was estimated as $20 billion. Spam is so cheap to send, that the breakeven conversion percentage has been estimated as 0.001% to 0.0001%.

It's again a business model with unit economics that lead to bad outcomes.

# Farms: Agricultural and Captcha

### Agricultural Farms

Farming has been around for 10,000 years but this old industry has gone through enormous change over the last century. A century ago farming was a significant part of the workforce of many countries, with the exception being places where farming was largely impractical, like Mongolia. In the US 100 years ago, agriculture was over one-third of employment. Today it is 2%. The global trend has been toward larger farms, run with larger fixed capital investments (tractors, harvesters, irrigation, drone surveillance and more). Data analysis, better crops, pesticides, and economies of scale have resulted in larger yields per acre.

Over the generations, farming scaled. Not to the extent of tech, but farmers produce much more on an acre of land currently than they could in the not so distant past. And unlike in the past, today there is generally plenty of food to go around. The problem now is more in distribution.

Farming is often thought of as stable, but is really dependent on a number of inputs that can change dramatically year to year. Is the weather good or bad for the crops grown? What happens to demand for crops? If selling internationally, what trade disputes might affect demand? What happens to the cost and availability of inputs, such as water for irrigation?

For staple crops, price swings of 50% in a year are common. Farmers can hedge against these potential risks and lock in a purchase price by buying a futures contract on the price of their crops they will later sell.

The idea for a government to set the price of food in order to avoid price gouging is also thousands of years old, with many examples from the Roman era. Likewise, government pushes to increase agricultural production are also known in history, where to attempt to meet demands of unrealistic scaling in China, people used theoretical agricultural practices such as deep plowing, lighting up outdoor fields at night, and using excessive fertilizer.

So what are the unit economics of farming? This is a complex question that varies by crop, subsidies, weather, demand and more.

This is another business type that seems simple, but is actually complicated. But I won't try to simplify this one. Instead, here are a few situations where policy and practice led to unusual outcomes.

Certain agricultural products became preferred because of their unit economics. Some examples:

- Hass Avocados became mainstream in part because their tougher skin helps them avoid bruising and look good as they come to market. Selling to distant customers became cheaper because of that.
- Strawberries have increased in size over the years. Strawberries must be picked by hand and so larger strawberries require less labor and cost less to produce.
- Subsidies for the dairy industry leads to excess milk production, which in turn leads to excess cheese production. The US has a stockpile of hundreds of thousands of tons of cheese.

## Captcha Farms

Captcha is an acronym for Completely Automated Public Turing test to tell Computers and Humans Apart. You've probably had to view and type or select the results of Captcha images when on certain sites. Captchas are used to distinguish humans from bots that spammers use for scalable website posting and contact detail scraping.

Captchas are also used by email providers to prevent spammers from automating account setup in order to quickly send spam messages from new, unblocked accounts. The Captcha makes account setup a bit too difficult for a computer and so a human has to be involved, at least at this point.

Captcha farms take Captchas and farm them out to people in low-income countries. These "farmers" work through the Captcha and type in their answers for a low payment. Their answers enable bots to access and spam the otherwise protected sites. The farms sell solved Captchas at around $1 to $2 per thousand. Captcha farmers (the people who solve them) work for about one-third to one-half of that fee.

A lot is required for this business to even be possible. First, the development of Captchas, which require humans to solve the puzzles, then volumes of farmers willing to work for very low wages, the spam industry business model which works even when adding the farming costs, and all the tech required to distribute the Captchas and answers.

# Scaling Gym Memberships and Fitness

The relatively traditional businesses of gyms and fitness studios have seen a few changes over the years.

These can be difficult businesses to grow. Revenue depends on people from a limited geographic area joining or visiting bricks-and-mortar locations. As a result, some gyms operate with member-to-available-space ratios of around 70 to 1 (70 members for every potential spot available in the gym). That is, they count on people not showing up in order for their business model to work. That's why many gyms don't stay in touch and remind you to come in to work out. They depend on low utilization.

Gyms and studios also deal with seasonality. Most members join at the beginning of the year and overall member retention can be less than half a year. They also have the difficulty (but also the opportunity) to charge different pricing for classes during peak and off-peak times.

Traditional factors to consider in these businesses include:
- Busy hour utilization. This is the real cap on memberships. Pre-COVID-19 this could be higher. It's also different based on whether the gym serves an office or residential population.
- How pricing impacts signups.
- Staffing the reception desk and providing instructors. Electricity, cleaning, rent, insurance, and more.
- Upfront capital costs for gym and other equipment that attracts and retains members.

That gives us:

*LTV of gym member = ((monthly membership fee + monthly purchase of other items like trainer time and food or drinks) - (cost to maintain the gym per member per month)) X number of months as members*

Let's look at how this model changes with ClassPass, a company that offers memberships granting access to fitness classes at a range of gyms, studios, and other formats.

A gym or studio listing on ClassPass can bring in more visitors but it also decreases the average price visitors pay. Also, gyms and studios using ClassPass may actually end up targeting a different customer segment that is not a fit for them long-term.

So a service like ClassPass can increase gym class attendance and lower CAC since it can target a large subscriber list. However, ClassPass also drives down fitness business LTV through forcing a lower price point and resulting in lower gym and studio member retention.

Early on, ClassPass started to sell an unlimited monthly class package at a rate lower than the amount they needed to pay out to the studios. While ClassPass ate that cost at first (it has raised $550 million total), it also trained gym-goers to expect low prices. The cynical view is that after enough gyms and studios were on ClassPass and dependent on that flow of students, ClassPass was able to reduce the fees they paid out to studios now dependent on their traffic. This is another situation where a highly funded company can insert itself into demand generation and eventually negatively impact the LTV of existing businesses.

It's a different situation from the mobility section. Taxi services don't think of passengers as retained -- there is no individual tracking and the fares are indistinguishable from each other. For Uber and Lyft, customer retention is essential and negative gross margin eventually has to improve. But there's no one else to push the costs to other than passengers and drivers. Gyms and studios previously had customer retention in that they formerly focused on selling memberships along with their own one-off drop-ins. But a move to ClassPass shifted retained gym and studio members to ClassPass members. And at a lower gross margin.

Whether ClassPass is overall beneficial to gyms and studios may be different case by case. But ClassPass apparently did improve one metric in the fitness industry -- retention. It's just that the retention improved was for their own customers, who pay monthly subscription fees.

Interestingly, during COVID-19, some attempts to force gyms to close merely drove their membership underground. The ideal gym fanatics would put up with sneaking into a speakeasy gym, paying higher membership fees, and potentially creating new ways to spread the disease. This is where small private gym operators can continue to offer service (even illegally) where ClassPass cannot.

# Cryptocurrency Mining

Mining is a process where cryptocurrency transactions are verified and added to the public blockchain ledger. Remaining competitive in this industry requires fast computers specialized to run this process.

Cryptocurrency mining necessarily takes a lot of computing power. As a comparison, processing one Bitcoin transaction requires thousands of times the energy needed to process one credit card transaction. That computing power takes a lot of electricity. That's why large cryptocurrency mining operations tend to be located near sources of cheap power (hydroelectric and solar), free power (college campuses and some apartment buildings), and where heat generated can be an asset rather than a cost.

Even if you run your mining operation efficiently, when the price paid for mining falls below the threshold of your costs, it stops making sense to mine the cryptocurrency. The price run that Bitcoin and many other cryptocurrencies saw for a few years, peaking in 2017 (at least at time of writing) led to a huge investment in mining operations. When prices fell, many of the computers used in those operations became junk, either sold at a huge discount or discarded.

Energy costs vary greatly by location, but a rough estimate from Digiconomist is that electricity accounts for 83% of the costs in a mining operation. A 17% gross margin can be a good business when done at large scale and without other significant costs. But this gross margin estimate varies with the difference in cryptocurrency prices and can be impossible to predict.

How can a cryptocurrency business reduce the largest part of its costs?

First, some mining operations locate themselves in places that are naturally cold. You may have seen news about houses that are heated by the excess heat thrown off by cryptocurrency mining rigs. This makes sense. Turn the generated heat -- which is the byproduct of electricity powering the machines -- into a cost savings or even an income stream.

Another way to deal with the cost of power is to locate the mining operation in a location that has cheap or free and plentiful power. Some notable operations are located by remote hydroelectric plants that are unable to sell all the electricity they produce.

As someone who works at a university, I've discovered first-hand another way people operate effectively. That is, locate the informal operation somewhere where the electricity cost is borne by someone else. I've personally discovered two mining operations based in university buildings. The quickest way to discover the owner is to unplug the rig.

# Fine Art: Where the Story Is

How do some visual artists sell their work? Often, they are represented by galleries. The galleries help them build a following among collectors, bring people together to see their work, represent the artists on the business side that they may otherwise do poorly, and more. For that, galleries typically take around 50% of the sale price as their fee.

Calculating CAC and LTV is difficult in such a business. Can the galleries adequately track the time and costs of cultivating talent and collectors over years?

Online art marketplaces like Saatchi Art may find that easier to do. Saatchi Art aggregates art buyers and artists. Artists upload images of their work and Saatchi Art takes a 35% commission of sales.

In traditional visual art, the highest priced sale of a painting goes to *Salvator Mundi*, by Leonardo da Vinci. But if you track the painting's price over time, you will find that it varied wildly over hundreds of years.

1500: da Vinci painted *Salvator Mundi*,
1651: the painting is sold for £30,

It appears to have been lost and forgotten as a work of da Vinci after this time. It shows up 300 years later.

1958: it's sold for £45,
2005: sold for $10,000.

A few years after this the painting was restored and again recognized as a work by da Vinci. Here's how the sales changed after this.

2013: sold for $75 million,
2013: sold for $127 million,
2017: and most recently it was sold for $450 million.

It's the same painting though.

At auction, where many high-priced artworks are resold, the auction house takes a fee for the sales.

Typical auction house fees are 12% of the price over $3 million, with higher percentages for works sold for less. In the case of *Salvator Mundi*, fees from the last sale were $50 million.

When collectors purchased *Salvator Mundi*, they didn't so much buy the image (which you can see online for free) as the story. The fact that it is attributed to da Vinci greatly adds to the price.

What people buy when they buy art is not necessarily what it seems. Especially in "modern" art, the story may be all of the value. If you don't know the story, you might not understand what is being purchased.

Another artist, Alejandro Cesarco made a conceptual piece called *Here Comes the Sun*.

This piece is conceptual because it is a list of directions for painting a yellow line across the baseboard of a wall. That's it. The materials needed to replicate this conceptual piece would only cost a few dollars.

CERTIFICATE

ALEJANDRO CESARCO
Here Comes the Sun, 2004
Yellow           on wall
Dimer              le
Editi

Making a duplicate would be trivial. That's why pieces like this also include a Certificate of Authenticity, issued by the art dealer. For a piece like *Here*

*Comes the Sun*, the certificate lists how many were made and what number this particular one is.

A work by the artist Banksy demonstrated the concept that buyers of some forms of art purchase stories rather than a physical product. At a Sotheby's auction, Banksy's work "Girl with Balloon" shredded itself in front of the crowd after purchase. (Banksy had earlier installed a shredder into the frame to be activated if the work were ever sold at auction.) That didn't matter though. If anything, shredding it increased the value.

At the other extreme is Dafen Village in China, which at its peak produced 60% of the oil paintings sold around the world, most of them copies of well-known originals. Painted by human artists, not replicated by printing, businesses of this type could grow, but not scale. Once a painter became expert at duplicating a masterpiece, they still needed similar time to paint each one.

A Dafen-replicated *Salvator Mundi* would not cost in the millions or even hundreds of thousands but merely in the hundreds of dollars at most. As far as I know, no one has duplicated *Here Comes the Sun*.

# App Stores and More: Controlling Payments

App stores manage several things for app developers. They manage distribution, hosting, uptime, identify viruses and malware, show user ratings, and handle payments. But because app access is through the app store and user information is not passed through, the user of an app has the more direct relationship with the app store itself, not the app developer.

For all of this, app stores take a fee from developers, typically 30% of revenue generated through their apps. For $0.99 apps, the most common price point after free, this 30% rate makes sense. It's what the app developer would have given up for payment processing anyway (typical credit card payment fees being 1.5% to 3% + $0.30).

Apple's agreement requires app developers to adhere to App Store terms, which includes provisions to exclude external payment processing for services delivered via the app. Free apps pay nothing apart from an annual developer fee. But there are some peculiarities to which app developers are charged.

Rideshare companies using Apple's App Store and Google Play provide their service off-app and so were judged as falling outside of the 30% fee rule.

Some other companies guard against the fee even when it means less sell-through. For example, Audible and Netflix do not enable purchases via their iOS app, Android app, or Amazon. The reason is to avoid the 30% fee that goes to those platforms.

These are called "reader apps." The App Store defines reader apps as apps that customers use to sign in to and read content from accounts they have already set up, even if they pay for it externally. From the App Store terms, reader apps: *"may allow a user to access previously purchased content or content subscriptions... provided that you agree not to directly or indirectly target iOS users to use a purchasing method other than in-app purchase, and your general communications about other purchasing methods are not designed to discourage use of in-app purchase."*

But, also for example, the $99/year Hey email app developed by Basecamp was blocked from Apple's App Store for not including an iOS subscription option. In other words, Apple blocked an app that didn't pass payments through the App Store, where Apple would receive 30%.

Apple's App Store and Google Play also both blocked Fortnite after the app offered users a discount to pay developer Epic Games directly, rather than via the app stores.

Do app stores take too much when they charge 30% of transaction value? Apple earned $50 billion from its App Store in 2019. Google earned $30 billion from Google Play in 2019. But other app stores, including those from Microsoft and Steam, have at times included modifications of the 30% at higher revenue volumes.

This is also a question of the trade-off between managing distribution, payments, security, and how subscription models change a business or app developers' willingness to part with large fees forever.

If you think of books as apps, a related example is Amazon's Kindle business. Many authors choose Kindle to distribute their books digitally, because that's where the readers are. But what fees does Amazon take to list and host a book?

The standard 30% (called the 70% royalty option) applies on certain price points -- $2.99 to $9.99. Outside of those prices, the rate changes to 65% (the 35% royalty option).

Additionally, Amazon charges a per sale delivery rate based on file size. Apart from the 30% (or 65%) per sale fee, the delivery fee to the author for selling this specific book is $0.22.

By working within an app store, the CAC for the app developer doesn't necessarily go away. Their apps still need to be discovered among the millions of options. But app developer LTV is impacted in different ways depending on price point. Since payment processing fees are typically 1.5% to 3% plus $0.30, apps that are cheap (free to $0.99) are not impacted or are cheaper to run on a typical app store. But for higher priced apps and especially for higher priced apps with subscriptions, a 30% fee builds up fast. Subscription models are going to force the app store issue in ways that my Kindle example (one off purchases) generally doesn't.

# Food Delivery: Harder Than It Used to Be

A few years ago we saw many highly funded food delivery startups emerge, grow, and then struggle or shutdown. A very short list of failed food delivery startups includes Munchery ($125 million raised), Sprig ($56.7 million raised), SpoonRocket ($13 million raised), and Maple ($25 million raised). What's so difficult about delivering food?

What's difficult is extrapolating what works locally and in a limited number of restaurant types to a growth model required by investors.

For example, Doubies ($670,000 raised) was a same-day cookie delivery service in the Bay area. The company apparently had good unit economics and was even net profitable, but was unable to grow. For venture-backed companies, running a small business is not an option. Doubies shut down.

Food delivery has been around for a long time, but when we have an industry shift in CAC and LTV driven by well-funded entrants that must show growth over good unit economics, strange things happen. A strategy that emerges is for well-funded but unsustainable businesses to price low and make survival expensive for competitors. Once the competitors shut down, the well-funded companies are the last ones standing. Maybe their CAC and LTV can improve afterward.

Even though food delivery might seem like a simple business, let's start by reminding ourselves of how it works. There's more going on than you might think.

To do delivery as a growth or scalable business, a company needs to manage:
- Offering either delivery of food from restaurants or food preparation and delivery of their own.
- For finished meals, getting the food from production to the customer in an acceptable time after ordering. For on-demand ordering this often means 30 minutes, or at least one hour or less. For scheduled ordering, this often means managing supply and demand.
- Keeping the food in a good condition during the delivery. This includes everything from packaging that can keep food at the appropriate temperature, keeping food presentable, including utensils if relevant, and more.
- Optimizing drivers and delivery routes.
- Integrating with legacy restaurant payment systems.

- Controlling payments so that customers pay the delivery service, which then pays the restaurant.
- Owning the customer experience, including web and in-app search.

Blue Apron ($199 million raised and IPO, which almost joined the food delivery deadpool list, has had a bit of a resurgence as COVID-19 made grocery shopping and going out to eat more difficult. Blue Apron, like Casper in the mattress section, loses money on every delivery. It has a positive gross margin on the food they prepare and sell (COGS of 61% to 71% for the past three years) but the other parts of its business make up for the rest of the loss, especially spending on "product, technology, general and administrative" which accounts for around 30% of revenue.

There are several ways to build food delivery businesses, but the modern ones that operate nationally do so with the assumption that there are benefits to operating a larger delivery business, including operational efficiencies, awareness driving customer usage, and market share power. But large size can be a weakness if it just means that the company loses money faster rather than succeed in a smaller market.

In general the food delivery model is hard. Companies deal with low customer order predictability, wasted ingredients, inability to optimize deliveries across wide areas, and high churn and high marketing costs.

So why does pizza delivery work? Pizza is generally made from a limited number of cheaper ingredients, quick to prepare and cooked when there are orders. Pizzas are prepared and delivered locally rather than nationally. Even the national pizza chains are really local businesses.

Also to compare, GrubHub, a business which does deliveries rather than also prepare the food, has similar economics to Blue Apron except with no cost of goods sold. DoorDash, another delivery business, takes 20% of the food order price as their fee, delivery fees (usually $5 to $8), and also earns revenue from selling advertising to restaurants (to appear higher in search results). DoorDash also sells a monthly subscription service in exchange for removing delivery fees.

These delivery services are not profitable either, but on a unit basis they're generally better than the national food delivery companies that also do the food preparation.

The large amount of investment dollars into food delivery skewed some parts of the business model. The small cookie delivery company above found that it needed to close down rather than continue to operate as a sustainable small business. But when well-funded companies need to show growth over unit economics it impacts other companies too. There are cases of delivery companies "hijacking" a restaurant's own search listings so that customers default to ordering through the delivery service. The result is less gross margin for the restaurants and also sometimes worse service (the negative reviews go to the restaurant, not the delivery service). A restaurant cares whether its food is delivered in good condition -- that affects its reputation. A delivery service that can push that cost to the restaurant will care less.

# Surveillance: Inevitable Outcomes of Progress

I include surveillance as case study because recently we've seen a growth both in surveillance devices (cameras and network equipment) but also more advances in facial recognition AI that enable surveillance of individuals and large groups. With increased device capabilities, declining costs, and improved software, this is a scalable business type.

But while we might understand the investment in surveillance technology for security (justified or unjustified), what are the potential business models around surveillance? There are a few. This section is mostly speculative at this time.

1. Invest in surveillance in order to reduce investment in corrective measures. That is, invest in surveillance tech that may help with crime prevention in order to reduce the costs to address crimes already committed. Actual data on this is spotty. In London, one example of a city that dramatically added surveillance tech, there has not been a match with crime reduction. Another extreme example is the implementation with various "social credit" scores in China with inputs coming from surveillance and other monitoring. These scores deliver penalties or benefits to individuals based on behavior.
2. Insurance-related benefits to surveillance tech implementation. For example, lower insurance premiums for installing home security systems.
3. Data collection unrelated to crime. This is potentially forward-looking and may lead to new insights. The ability to better understand human movement, social differences, changes in demand, healthcare, and other non-crime issues.

The world is moving in this direction.

As surveillance tech becomes cheaper, it seems to be deployed regardless of effect on crime prevention or accuracy of criminal identification. That is, whatever the use case, cameras, sensors, and software systems drop in price to the point at which there need not be a strong business case.

Similar to the file storage section above, the cost to provide devices, storage, and analysis move in one direction -- down. Eventually, this impacts how governments, companies, and individuals make decisions.

At least, that's the potential that seems to be playing out. We'll see.

# Ending Note

I hope that you have found this book helpful and will use it as a reference when thinking through CAC, LTV, retention, cohorts, and other issues.

To write this book I drew upon my work with startups and teaching over years. However, I put it all together during the COVID-19 pandemic.

That office sign I mentioned in the introduction now goes unseen by everyone. But I hope that you will find ways to see and discover regardless of where you are.

To stay in touch about *Growth Units*, send an email to this address: paul@startupsunplugged.com

Courage.

# Glossary

**Bookings**: The value of customer contracts, not necessarily what customers actually do pay.

**Business Model**: The way a business creates value, captures value, and incurs costs to provide that value.

**Business Model - Direct**: The business sells directly to its customers.

**Business Model - Indirect**: The business provides a service that attracts unpaid users and then sells access to those users (typically advertising or data revenue streams).

**Business Model - Marketplace**: The business matches buyers and sellers of products and services and take a fee for doing so.

**CAC**: Customer acquisition cost. A measure of the costs required to turn a non-customer into a customer.

**Captcha**: Completely Automated Public Turing test to tell Computers and Humans Apart. Captchas often require a user to type in the text of difficult to read letters and numbers or to solve a math problem.

**Churn**: A measure of how customers or users leave. Often presented per time period or cohort.

**COGS**: Cost of Goods Sold.

**Contribution Margin**: The price of the product or service minus the variable costs to product the product or service.

**CPM**: Cost per thousand. This is an advertising term for the cost to show an ad to 1,000 people.

**Discount Rate**: A collection of assumptions about risk used to modify the value of future payments.

**Fixed Costs**: Costs that are relatively fixed and do not move up or down in line with new customers or usage. These costs do however tend to move up or down in steps.

**Gross Margin**: The portion of revenue that is left after subtracting costs required for the production of a unit of product. This is normally used on a business level, not an individual customer level. Gross Margin is presented as a ratio while Gross Profit is presented as a fixed dollar amount.

**Gross Profit**: The fixed dollar amount left over after subtracting unit costs from revenue. This is normally used on a business level, not an individual customer level. Gross Profit and Gross Margin refer to the same thing.

**Growth**: Getting larger as determined by additional customers, revenue, gross margin/gross profit, or service area.

**Ideal or "Earlyvangelist" Customers**: The people who most benefit from a company's products, especially in the beginning.

**LTV**: Lifetime Value. A measure of the gross profit a business earns from a customer over time. The components of LTV are price, cost, and retention.

**Negative Churn**: Negative churn is based on revenue or gross margin, not customers. A smaller number of customers on average pay more to the point that it results in higher per overall revenue (the additional revenue more than makes up for the lost customers). You may also see negative churn referred to as positive net revenue retention.

**Network Effects**: The way some products and services gain value when more people use them.

**Operating Margin**: Gross margin minus R&D, overhead, administrative, and operational expenses such as rent, payroll, benefits, insurance, and utilities.

**Retention**: A measure of how long a customer keeps buying or how many times they buy from a business. Also a measure of how long users stay with an unpaid service.

**Revenue**: Payments customers generate for the business. Recognized when the service is provided.

**Scalable**: Growth that improves in efficiency, either by reducing costs per customer or increasing revenue or gross margin per customer.

**Variable Costs**: Costs that move up or down with the increase or decrease in customer usage.

# Selected Sources

This is a selection of the sources noted throughout the book.

Customer Acquisition Cost
*Four Steps to the Epiphany*, Steve Blank
The Money and Math Behind Our Newsletter Headlines, CB Insights
Ferrari NV Annual Report, 2015
Google Ads Benchmarks for Your Industry, Wordstream
Frequently Asked Questions about Small Business, SBA

Lifetime Value
Social apps with highest retention rate, Statista
Why Everything I Thought I Knew About Churn Is Wrong, Tomasz Tunguz
West Side Rag » Gray's Papaya Just Reopened With an Extra-Special
Recession Special

Mattresses: Bricks-and-Mortar and Online
Are We in a Mattress-Store Bubble? (Ep. 251) - Freakonomics
Casper - Reports & Filings
How Mattress Markets Are Changing in Stores and Online, EconLife
The War To Sell You A Mattress Is An Internet Nightmare, Fast Company
Inside Casper's Financials — The Information

Subscription and Freemium: Data Storage, Movies, and More
Why Movie Theaters Should Applaud MoviePass — The Information
Behind the math of MoviePass, the $10-a-month movie subscription
service that sounds too good to be true, Recode

Mobility: Taxi Medallions, Rideshare, Scooters, and Bikes
How Uber Makes — And Loses — Money, CB Insights
Micro Mobility Revolution: Startups, Companies & Market Solutions, CB
Insights
Using Big Data to Estimate Consumer Surplus: The Case of Uber, NBER
Uber's IPO Is Historic, Despite Its $10 Billion Loss, The Atlantic
Inside Bird's Scooter Economics — The Information
Scooters might actually have good unit economics, Oversharing
How long does a scooter last? Less than a month, Louisville data
suggests, QZ

Consumer Packaged Goods (CPG)
Supermarkets "Rigged" through Secret Deals with Food Manufacturers,
Cspinet

Ecommerce: Centralizing Supply and Demand
US Ecommerce 2020, Emarketer

Returns: A Byproduct
We entered the multi-million dollar business behind your Amazon returns,
Yahoo! Finance
How to Sell Amazon Liquidation Pallets, The Atlantic

Organized Crime: Illegal Drug Trade
From Colombia to New York City: The narconomics of cocaine, Business
Insider
Illegal Drugs and Coronavirus, Unintended Consequences blog

Parasites: Ransomware and Spam
Garmin Hack and Dependence, Unintended Consequences blog
Business Model of a Botnet

Farms: Agricultural and Captcha
Total Market Profitability by quarter, Gross, Operating and Net Margin from
2 Q 2020, CSI Market
Food from Thought, Unintended Consequences blog

Scaling Gym Memberships and Fitness
Secret Gyms And The Economics Of Prohibition : Planet Money
At some gyms, the New Year's set keeps memberships longest, Second
Measure
ClassPass Is Squeezing Fitness Studios 'To the Point of Death', Vice

Cryptocurrency Mining
Bitcoin Energy Consumption Index, Digiconomist

Fine Art: Where the Story Is
For Love or Money, the Merits of Investing In Art, The Easel
One of Banksy's paintings self-destructed just after it was auctioned, The
Verge
Banksy video: https://www.instagram.com/p/BomXijJhArX/

This Village Used to Make 60% of the World's Paintings—Now Its Future Is in Jeopardy, Artsy
Apple App Store had estimated gross sales of $50 billion in 2019, CNBC
*Here Comes the Sun* certificate of authenticity photo by the author

App Stores and More: Controlling Payments
Apple Threatens to Remove Email App 'Hey' From App Store Over Lack of In-App Subscription Option, Mac Rumors
Apple approves Hey email app, but the fight's not over, The Verge
Apple Developer Guidelines, Apple
Digital Pricing Page, Amazon Kindle

Food Delivery: Harder Than It Seems
After raising $125M, Munchery fails to deliver, TechCrunch
Doughbies' cookie crumbles in a cautionary tale of venture scale, TechCrunch
Once in a Blue Apron, Startups Unplugged

Surveillance: Inevitable Outcomes of Progress
Inevitable Surveillance? Unintended Consequences blog

**Lastly, thank you to:**
SJ, CF, EJ, TA, SF, CL, RT, FP

Printed in the USA
CPSIA information can be obtained
at www.ICGtesting.com
LVHW051542080124
768383LV00003B/455

9 798678 691996